Copyright © 2020

All rights reserved. This book or any portion thereof may not be reproduced or used in any manner whatsoever without the express written permission of the publisher except for the use of brief quotations in a book review or scholarly journal.

Special thanks to Erica Stall Wiggins for her help in putting this book together

First Printing: 2020

SHOCKORAMA BOOKS INC.
4425 SOUTH MOPAC EXPRESSWAY
SUITE 601, AUSTIN, TX 78738

This type in this book is set in Garamond.

The Poetry Machine

Volume No. 1

SHOCKORAMA BOOKS

The Poetry Machine

Many years ago now, I was having a conversation with J.W. Nickles and we were lamenting the fact that our poetry output had waned in our thirties to an almost nonexistent trickle. We decided that night to commit to writing a poem each week using a random prompt as a starting point, and started to invite other creative types along for the ride. Some of the contributors to this book make their living in the field of music, or acting or photography. There are lawyers, and graphic designers. Film makers and layabouts. Very few if any make their living writing, but they all share one thing in common. The joy of creating. Here is a sampling of some of their work from the past few years of the Poetry Machine.

Please to enjoy,
Bob Schneider

Karl Anderson	1
Karl Anderson	2
Karl Anderson	3
Karl Anderson	4
ONE MORE MORNING	*4*
Karl Anderson	5
I MIGHT EVEN BUY ONE	*5*
Ted Beck	6
69	*6*
Ted Beck	7
FYC	*7*
Ted Beck	8
IGLOO GRAFFITI	*8*
Ted Beck	10
Marci	*10*
Ted Beck	12
WORTH A DAMN	*12*
Hayes Carll	14
THE LIFEGUARD	*14*
George Carver	15
Like Old Men	*15*
George Carver	16
Outcomes	*16*
George Carver	17
Simple Ambitions	*17*
George Carver	18
Velvet Cage	*18*
Tyler Reed Cochran	19

    As Nightfall Came 19
TYLER REED COCHRAN 20
    One more morning for the Prince of Darkness 20
TYLER REED COCHRAN 21
    One Thing I Know 21
TYLER REED COCHRAN 22
    This Collection of Junk 22
JOHN CUSIMANO 23
    I MIGHT EVEN BUY ONE 23
JOHN CUSIMANO 24
    I WAS 16 24
JOHN CUSIMANO 25
    THE AFTERLIFE 25
JOHN CUSIMANO 26
    THE WHOLE BUSINESS 26
JOHN CUSIMANO 27
    TOO MANY BOATS 27
TATE DONOVAN 28
TATE DONOVAN 29
TATE DONOVAN 30
TATE DONOVAN 31
    The Barkeep 31
TATE DONOVAN 32
JODI EGERTON 33
JODI EGERTON 34
JODI EGERTON 35
    FOR EMILY, WHENEVER I MAY FIND HER 35
JODI EGERTON 36
JODI EGERTON 37

OWEN EGERTON 38
OWEN EGERTON 39
OWEN EGERTON 40
OWEN EGERTON 41
OWEN EGERTON 42
FONDA FISHER 43
   AT THE END OF THE SEA *43*
FONDA FISHER 44
   BRING CLOUDS *44*
FONDA FISHER 45
   GUILLOTINE *45*
FONDA FISHER 46
   THE ITCH *46*
FONDA FISHER 48
   THROUGH THE FLAMES *48*
MARK GROCHOWSKI 49
   discontinued beauty *49*
MARK GROCHOWSKI 50
   hold still *50*
MARK GROCHOWSKI 51
   to love for saving mE *51*
MARK GROCHOWSKI 52
   nightmare radio *52*
MARK GROCHOWSKI 53
   once upon a time *53*
JASON Z GUEST 54
   CANDIED CORAL CRUSH *54*
JASON Z GUEST 55
   CHANNEL HATE *55*

JASON Z GUEST 56
   CROSSING THE LINE.. 56
JASON Z GUEST 57
   MORE TIME 57
JASON Z GUEST *THE HEIR* 58
CHRIS HANNIGAN 60
   GOOD FOR THE SOUL 60
CHRIS HANNIGAN 61
   MY HOME OF LOVE 61
CHRIS HANNIGAN 63
   THE THIEF IN ME 63
CHRIS HANNIGAN 64
   WITHIN MILES 64
CHRIS HANNIGAN 65
   WHO KNOWS? 65
BILLY HARVEY 66
   ACROSS THE ROAD 66
BILLY HARVEY 67
   GENE WILDER 67
BILLY HARVEY 68
   HOME 68
BILLY HARVEY 69
   PIROUETTE 69
BILLY HARVEY 70
   THE ONLY ONE 70
MARGARET HELTZEL 71
   3/4's FINISHED 71
MARGARET HELTZEL 72
   ALL THE DIFFERENCE 72

Margaret Heltzel 73
   I WOULD BE LOST 73
Margaret Heltzel 74
   THIS COLLECTION OF JUNK 74
Margaret Heltzel 75
   WHEN LOVE BEGINS 75
Bruce Hughes 76
   DANCING WITH SWANELLE 76
Bruce Hughes 77
   FERAL 77
Bruce Hughes 78
   HOW THE ELEGANT FOWL LOST ITS DESIRE TO SING 78
Bruce Hughes 79
   MOON STUFF 79
Lauren Jahnke 80
Lauren Jahnke 81
Lauren Jahnke 82
Lauren Jahnke 83
Guy Juke 84
   A POETRY MACHINE 84
Guy Juke 85
   DISTURBING THE DUST 85
Guy Juke 87
Guy Juke 88
   REFLEX ERECTION 88
Guy Juke 89
   TOUCHING COMPUTER KEYS: 89
Andrew Long 91
   DEATH SHALL NOT DO US PART 91

ANDREW LONG 92
    LOOK 92
ANDREW LONG 93
    NEW MEXICO SUMMER OF '78 93
ANDREW LONG 94
    ONE TWENTY SQUARE 94
ANDREW LONG 96
    ONLY 96
GARETH MAGUIRE 97
    A NICE THOUGHT SURE WOULD FEEL GOOD 97
GARETH MAGUIRE 98
    HANGING ON UPSIDE DOWN 98
GARETH MAGUIRE 99
    IN MY HOUSE 99
GARETH MAGUIRE 100
    IN OTHER COUNTRIES 100
GARETH MAGUIRE 101
    STUDENT OF DREAMS 101
TIM MCKEE 102
    Ebb and Flow 102
TIM MCKEE 103
TIM MCKEE 104
    The Grey 104
TIM MCKEE 105
    The Sweet 105
TIM MCKEE 106
SETH MEEKS 107
    CBD 107
SETH MEEKS 108

Denim Sheets 108
SETH MEEKS 109
   Grackle Jackson 109
SETH MEEKS 110
   16 110
SETH MEEKS 111
   Us Against Death 111
FELIX MORGAN 113
   As Nightfall Came 113
FELIX MORGAN 114
   Fox and Crow 114
FELIX MORGAN 115
   Ici tout est bon 115
FELIX MORGAN 117
   Love in the time of COVID-19 117
FELIX MORGAN 118
   The moon and the wind 118
MICHAEL NATTER 119
   3/4's Finished 119
MICHAEL NATTER 120
   A Bad Winter 120
MICHAEL NATTER 121
   Bughouse 121
MICHAEL NATTER 122
   Silver Fish 122
MICHAEL NATTER 123
   What's your name? 123
NANCY NATTER 124
   Chivalry is Dead 124

NANCY NATTER 125
    NiGht Stalking *125*

NANCY NATTER 126
    Walls *126*

NANCY NATTER 127
    With A Smile *127*

NANCY NATTER 128
    With His Tongue *128*

J.W. NICKLES 129
    Interview with Anna Akhmatova *129*

J.W. NICKLES 130
    Interview with George Balanchine *130*

J.W. NICKLES 131
    Interview with Sofia Kovalevskaya *131*

J.W. NICKLES 133
    Vladimir for Vera *133*

NINA OTAZO 134
    Blame *134*

NINA OTAZO 135
    Demented *135*

NINA OTAZO 136
    EAR TO THE GROUND *136*

NINA OTAZO 137
    Que Sera *137*

NINA OTAZO 138
    Tossing in My Sleep *138*

GREGORY PAGE 139
    A TRUE GRAMOPHONE POEM *139*

GREGORY PAGE 140

ONE HELL OF A SMELL	140
GREGORY PAGE	141
THE OWL & THE SQUIRREL	141
GREGORY PAGE	142
THE POTATO EATERS	142
GREGORY PAGE	143
THE TRUE MEANING OF OPTIMISM	143
DARREN PATNODE	144
Austin 1991	144
DARREN PATNODE	145
DARREN PATNODE	146
DARREN PATNODE	147
you and i half hearted	147
TURK PIPKIN	148
A River Deep	148
TURK PIPKIN	149
Fragante Delecti	149
TURK PIPKIN	150
Little Man	150
TURK PIPKIN	152
The Firefly	152
TURK PIPKIN	153
Thief of Hearts	153
TURK PIPKIN	154
True Love	154
TED ROBERSON	155
A DUMP LIKE THIS	155
TED ROBERSON	156
BLACKLUNG SUN	156

TED ROBERSON 157
   MY EYES ARE BROKEN SEEDS *157*
TED ROBERSON 158
   OH, THAT GOAL *158*
TED ROBERSON 159
   TOILET *159*
CHARLES ROCHA 160
CHARLES ROCHA 161
CHARLES ROCHA 162
CHARLES ROCHA 163
CHARLES ROCHA 164
REY ROCHA 165
REY ROCHA 166
REY ROCHA 167
REY ROCHA 168
REY ROCHA 169
JAMES ROTONDI 170
JAMES ROTONDI 171
JAMES ROTONDI 172
JAMES ROTONDI 173
JAMES ROTONDI 174
ALI SALZMANN 175
   Belief *175*
ALI SALZMANN 176
   Good for the Soul *176*
ALI SALZMANN 177
   Headed to El Paso at the End of the World *177*
ALI SALZMANN 178
   Morning *178*

BLU SANDERS 179
   DID IT END? *179*
BLU SANDERS 180
   FACE THE SUN *180*
BLU SANDERS 181
   FAR ABOVE THE WORLD *181*
BLU SANDERS 182
   OLD SCARS *182*
BLU SANDERS 183
   SET FIRE TO THE STARS *183*
BOB SCHNEIDER 184
   EL NEGRO *184*
BOB SCHNEIDER 185
   ITS HARD TO WRITE A GOOD SONG THESE DAYS *185*
BOB SCHNEIDER 186
   MAYBE I COULD BE HAPPY *186*
BOB SCHNEIDER 187
   STAR SMOKE *187*
BOB SCHNEIDER 189
   THUNDERBALL *189*
BOB SCHNEIDER SR. 192
   A DARK SUIT *192*
BOB SCHNEIDER SR. 193
   AND SHE WILL *193*
BOB SCHNEIDER SR. 194
   IN THE AFTERNOON *194*
BOB SCHNEIDER SR. 195
   INTO THE DISTANCE *195*
BOB SCHNEIDER SR. 196

NOTHING WITHOUT END	196
JORDAN STONE	197
JORDAN STONE	198
JORDAN STONE	199
JORDAN STONE	200
JORDAN STONE	201
ANDREW SWENSEN	202
Assateague	*202*
ANDREW SWENSEN	203
"Life and Almost Life"	*203*
ANDREW SWENSEN	205
"Love in the Time of Corona." A Sonnet	*205*
ANDREW SWENSEN	206
"The Art of Forgetting"	*206*
ANDREW SWENSEN	207
"The Monster In the Walls"	*207*
JEFF SWENSEN	208
JEFF SWENSEN	209
JEFF SWENSEN	210
JEFF SWENSEN	211
JEFF SWENSEN	212
JIM WALKER	213
10/3/18	*213*
JIM WALKER	214
4/10/19	*214*
JIM WALKER	215
5/9/19	*215*
JIM WALKER	216
6/26/19	*216*

JIM WALKER	217
4/8/20	*217*
WAMMO	218
I faked my own life	*218*
WAMMO	219
motherwell	*219*
WAMMO	222
Re: Monetize	*222*
WAMMO	225
TEN ROTTEN POEMS ABOUT OMAR SHARIF	*225*
WAMMO	228
Uni	*228*
JARED WARREN	232
JARED WARREN	233
JARED WARREN	234
JARED WARREN	235
JARED WARREN	236
ERICA STALL WIGGINS	237
An Island	*237*
ERICA STALL WIGGINS	238
CHRISTMAS CARDS	*238*
ERICA STALL WIGGINS	239
First Day of School	*239*
ERICA STALL WIGGINS	240
GOODWILL	*240*
ERICA STALL WIGGINS	241
THE AAA BALL GAME	*241*
HAROLD WHIT WILLIAMS	242
A Few Lines For Those I Love	*242*

HAROLD WHIT WILLIAMS	243
Made For TV	*243*
HAROLD WHIT WILLIAMS	244
Sad Ballad of Elsewhere	*244*
HAROLD WHIT WILLIAMS	245
Sentimental Hogwash	*245*
HAROLD WHIT WILLIAMS	246
Silent Witness	*246*
CHAPIN WILSON	247
CHAPIN WILSON	248
CHAPIN WILSON	249
CHAPIN WILSON	250
CHAPIN WILSON	251
DAVID WILSON	252
BOB DYLAN HAS DIED	*252*
DAVID WILSON	254
CIVIL WAR PHOTO	*254*
DAVID WILSON	256
SOMETHING RICH AND STRANGE	*256*

Karl Anderson

I lie down in the shadow
and do snow angels
but the shadow
is not snow
        it's an oil-
black whisper
that gives most people the chills
but I roll around
with it like I'm playing
with a big, friendly dog.

Karl Anderson

I live on the outskirts of town
on the edge of town
where the wilderness starts.
It makes sense for my
position
in the community to be
staked out here.

After all, I am the sheriff.
And the sheriff watches over.

In some cultures my
title would be shaman.
I like sheriff, but
it's all just words, though.
It's all just ideas
that creates vibrations
so which exact word
doesn't matter.

I live on the outskirts of town
where the wilderness starts
because
I understand how the border
works.
All the difference between
the two sides is
a thin whisper.
A thought. A feeling.
A feeling that gives us ideas
on what to do about
the strange sounds.
A vibration
    We all must answer to.

Karl Anderson

I was 16 feet tall when the cops
first started messing with me.
They didn't like the way I looked,
like I was up to no good, they said.
They said it was the way I dressed,
but I could tell it was that they were
all straining their necks looking up
to me, and they didn't like that.

At 18 feet, having applied first to the CIA
to be an undercover man, they suggested
I join the circus. They said they liked me,
but they couldn't do anything formal with me
cause of my height and all, but that I should
be on the lookout for malevolent forces
behind the scenes under the big top,
and to report to them at once if I'd heard
or seen any of these.
I didn't last long at the circus. I got run out
by a group of midgets who said I was snooping around too much.

I peaked at 19 1/2 feet when the General
of an intergalactic alien task force
asked me to join their team of cleaning up
all the unnecessary plastic floating out
in space and slowing down their thoroughfares. You'd be amazed
how much is out there.
I like the job, it keeps me busy and my
longer than average arms allow me to reach
stuff most people need a ladder to get to.

Karl Anderson

ONE MORE MORNING

Someone gave me coffee.
It might not have been the
best idea.
I was notorious for getting excited
on coffee.

Then they suggested smoothies.

"Well," I said, "It wouldn't hurt."

(Time passed. The landscape was
   generous.)

And then there were a couple
 of parades
and crowns were being
handed out.
I had a great relationship with
the wine steward,
I can tell you that.

It looked like everything
was going perfectly over the next
several weeks, months, years,
decades
and then one more morning
happened and the maidens
were bringing me mimosas
and over of them
whispered
that if I were smart,
I'd take a match to the whole thing.

Oh! Coffee! You silly bitch.

Karl Anderson

I MIGHT EVEN BUY ONE

What would you pay?
For a poem to come to you
in the middle of the night
that's actually
the very
ridiculous
notion
that God is coming
to you
     as a favor.

Ted Beck

69

I quit drinking on
my mother's 69th birthday
It was my gift to her
and yet at the very same time
It was for me

However
I can't just lie back and enjoy it
I gotta put the work in
so I can really lick this thing--
Once and for all!

Ted Beck

FYC

sitting dirty on the grass in the front yard
shooting my dog in the face with a cap gun
slim jim between my lips like a meat cigarette
so many delicious boogers in my nose
When my dad's black mercedes rolled into the cul de sac
he was listening to Fine Young Cannibals
And still wearing his stethoscope
I hid behind the tree I 'd carved "ASS" in

sharks swam in the dirt beneath my feet

stuck in the tree above was a black yellow football
i threw my gun into the branches til the ball fell at my feet
it was heavy with water, skin cracked from the cold
i slit my fingernail along the surface, cutting it open
then plunged my finger deep into the Nerfy meat
it was tight and wet and the foam formed to my finger
i dug in further and further, now with my whole hand
thrilled to be destroying something i'd forgotten

sharks swam in the dirt beneath my feet

Ted Beck

IGLOO GRAFFITI

Trotting all over Arctic tundra
through lands made of glass
and colors one has only seen in
experimental Gatorade flavors—
I realized I was super, very lost.
I was beyond meat and so hungry.
Also, my coat? Soppy to the max.

I howled when I saw the dome,
milky and sparkling yonder.
Run, run, run to it, I did.
Then burrow, burrow, pause, burrow—
until I found myself in the cool womb,
the wind put on mute.
My eye adjusted to the murky to see
the walls were covered in igloo graffiti.

I read some and snickered,

"I lost a mitten in Yuka's kitten"
"Inuit quim = fishing hole"
"You are what you eat— I am the walrus"
"Fartfuck"
"Tiguaak has small pox"

But the last one was most curious.

"Kanook sucked my meat popsicle,
then Kanook licked my frozen balls
with her wet pink tongue and
it got stuck…"

Had to cock head, use my nails
to scratch away extra frost.

The message went on:

"Kanook screamed from
the way back of her throat
so I yanked her head of
oil black hair, making her tongue
stretch like blubber.
I fear she will be stuck there.
She will not survive the endless winter.
She will die on my sac,
this fissured bag that makes life
will in time offer her death.
Even now, as I write this, she is
screaming, pulling, making ice tears.
Ah yes, yes, yes, Kanook.
My moment of ecstasy will be
frozzen [sic] in time."

I turned to the skeletons
pretzeled behind me—
skull stuck to pelvis,
other skull smiling.
The graffiti was super accurate.
My penis exited my fur and
I felt like an evil, sick dog.
Pushed penis into snow
so it could disappear.

Whimpering, sad for all, I used my
thorny teeth to gnash free
a Kanook foot bone,
then ran the shit outta there,
back out onto da tundra
with my misty pants—
paws crunching snow,
jaws crunching toe!

Ted Beck

MARCI

News of an ex-girlfriends suicide came in excited,
sad faced texts
This was the third one in as many months
I had to reactivate my Facebook to read the remembrances
My own weren't fit to print:

Marci sitting Indian style, yawning
before my spread open legs
With teeth the size of business cards,
Elephant/flower tattoos
And that blonde unambition

How we spent that whole summer looking like
fresh glazed donuts
Hickeys ringing her neck
Breached pillow barriers, margarita madness,
the Strokes still working on us
And the time she tried to quit smoking
moaning, "This just isn't worth it"

If Aunt Ashley was here she would point to the sky
and show me which bird you are
A cardinal or pigeon, maybe
Or probably the one who just
flew right into my glass window
And now lies sideways on the sill
Twitching as the worms rejoice.

Why didn't you call me?
I mean, text.
Why didn't you text me?

I wonder who cut you down
What you were wearing

If you cried as you tied the bathrobe sash or
If it was the happiest you'd ever be
And if after, your dogs had enough time
to take a bite out of you.

Delicious you.

Ted Beck

WORTH A DAMN

The empty house
Back home in the living room
my dad wants to know who
Rosamund Pike is
"Who's this Rosamund Pike?
Is she worth a damn?"
He's on a couch, I'm on another
A stethoscope lies coiled on the coffee table
Next to a coffee table book about decaf

Outside on the deck
the fountain looks like
It's dribbling clear gelatin
Like the stuff you'd find in a cyst
It's been raining a lot
"We needed it"
And the yard looks like a
Hi-def Easter basket
There are bunnies, cardinals, squirrels,
Bluebirds, foxes and a black guy
With a chainsaw
Brilliant nature

White sunlight streams through the trees
Onto the black dogs back
Making her look like a barcode
Later we'll stand in a semi circle
And quietly rub ointment on its vagina
Our sweatshirt hoods over our heads
Like some sort of ancient ritual
As we spell out the words B-A-L-L
And C-A-R and O-I-N-T-M-E-N-T
I take a sip of cold Folgers and
To my father I say,

"She was in Gone Girl"
He sucks in his lips, takes this in...
A thought flashes across his
Wizard, puppet face
Then with alarm he asks,
"Where is your mother?"

Hayes Carll

THE LIFEGUARD

the two freckled teenage twins frolicked in the swimming pool
laughing and carrying on with each other under the August sun
boys
I liked them
well, one of them
one of them was a shit but I could never tell them which
they both ate cheeseburgers and hotdogs that day
and being twins they went under at the same time
I jumped down from my post and ran to apply suntan lotion to
Mrs. Germanium
on the wind I heard my dad proudly whisper
"that was the only life you could save."

George Carver

LIKE OLD MEN

Sometimes the waves of feeling are so powerful
Just sitting in the garage waiting for the grill to heat up
It's raining just a little
Cold in a thin wife beater
I watch people walking down to the YMCA and think
Sha la la la la la la la la………..
Here I am now
Like old men all around the world
Maybe a slivovitz at breakfast
Along with tears and memories

George Carver

OUTCOMES

Between concerns about the outcomes
And fears about the process little gets done
Deference fills the void
Nobody is off to the races and I'm standing here
Pockets full of comas and semi colons
Adjective, allusion, command of form and language
A pool of tears evaporating over the uneven surface of life
Little girls laughing at me as I walk down the street
Every time I hear the words neruda or borges
There is some echo in the room
A standing wave
Plaster walls, chipped and stained
The hair of the horses in the lath was run through the pampas
The mouse dung behind the base boards was grain from Italy
All this connected by the wind that runs through the cracks
All part of some song some poem some words

George Carver

SIMPLE AMBITIONS

Simple ambitions
A hot bath and maybe some ice cream
If I were to live my life with some other frame of mind
Maybe there would be other things
Her love is a simple thing, without adornment
without aspiration she comes, to simply put me in her arms
The future, the past, and the present are all here
To find love is a simple ambition
To gain love is no simple accomplishment

George Carver

VELVET CAGE

In the velvet cage
Alone
Soft breezes and happy sunlight
The bars might even drift into imagination
Reverie is short
The children call up from the street
Admonishing me for age and experience
They need answers but will not open the door
Sometimes you laugh alone
In the velvet cage

Tyler Reed Cochran

AS NIGHTFALL CAME

The weight of your words
The way your multi-color barretts playfully pin your hair
and my name feels safe in your mouth
The way you hold back the sun
with an air of frisky forgetfulness
like a devilish, flippant prank
The world needs your permission
so I ask gently
to let myself drown in your negligence
knowing it will sufficiently cover every error
and allow for everything
all-at-once
to be smothered in your honor

Tyler Reed Cochran

ONE MORE MORNING FOR THE PRINCE OF DARKNESS

We stopped working but the Devil didn't
he's been rolling his favorite number
marking beasts and microchipping tech employees
burying souls six feet deep
riding the Shock Wave at Six Flags
and making six inch meatball subs.

Beezelbub doesn't care
about your political opinion
or your latest FB post
he's busy hitting Broadway for Six the Musical
using his six inch voice in the classroom
and reading the tabloids on Page Six.

We've been wearing masks
while his has been removed
and he's not abiding by the six foot separation
but pulling the Six of Cups in his latest Tarot reading
and trying new recipes on Six Sisters' Stuff
the best pumpkin honey bun cake is his seasonal favorite.

Tyler Reed Cochran

ONE THING I KNOW

It's true what they say
things like 'nothing lasts forever'
and 'cherish every moment because you don't know how many
you have left'
It's true that in every life a little rain must fall
even in San Diego
and we should live every day like it's our last
It turns out it's all true
God and Jesus and the Holy Spirit
and Mary and Joseph and the three wise men
and Michael and the devil and demons and heaven and hell
It's true we will find peace at last
and we will lie in the grass with a smile on our faces
but first we will have tribulation on this earth
It's true you shouldn't judge others
and you should walk a mile in their shoes
uphill both ways in the snow
and you should brush your teeth at night and once in the
morning and floss
and tell every single person you love them
and turn the other cheek
and turn newborns so their heads shape correctly
It's true that smoking kills
and that sticks and stones will break your bones
but I've felt words hurt
more than anything else

Tyler Reed Cochran

THIS COLLECTION OF JUNK

The Lizards want their throne back
dolls without voodoo
riding seahorses
and eating poached bald eagle eggs
like ancient Mesopotamian demons

John Cusimano

I MIGHT EVEN BUY ONE

I was walking through Chinatown
And saw a case of stinky, smelly, rotten century eggs
I thought I might even buy one
And I did

I was sitting at a Sushi bar in downtown Hiroshima
And I saw shirako – which is fish sperm -- in the sushi case
I thought I might even eat some
And I did

I was drunk in a shanty in Cambodia
And saw terrifying, nightmare inspiring, crispy tarantulas on the daily specials
I thought I might even try one
And I did

I was hanging in Yellowknife, Canada to watch the auroras
And a local gent offered me a small delicate plate of jellied moose nose
I was hungry anyway and quite numb, so I decided to try one
And I did

I was in Sardinia once, on a boat
And someone's sweet leather faced Italian grandmother insisted I eat her homemade Casu Marzu
(Casu Marzu is rotten cheese with live maggots squirming around the cheese)
(It smells like the most disgusting toilet you've ever had to use)
(Times ten)
I was really really hungry that day
And I thought I might even eat some
But I didn't

John Cusimano

I WAS 16

I smoked pot and freaked out and drank blackberry brandy and got in trouble with the law and may have stolen some ground meats and may have pushed over a pickle barrel or two and I have a vague recollection of a hit and run but I don't think anyone died and that may or may not have been in a stolen car but I was planning on returning the car after I stole it but I smashed up that car pretty badly and then for no reason at all I went to Denny's at 1am and threw everyone's pancakes on the floor and laughed maniacally and ran away and went to prom and burned the entire gymnasium down using telekinesis and robbed a bank and went to 7-11 and broke the slurpee machine and there was cherry slurpee spewing everywhere and it was the funniest thing ever and then someone tackled me and then I blacked out.
But I was 16, so it was OK.

John Cusimano

THE AFTERLIFE

I imagine the afterlife
As a party where
Everyone has a full glass of gin
And you drink too much
And get sick
But then everyone cleans up everyone else's mess

John Cusimano

THE WHOLE BUSINESS

As I stared at my pocket watch through the smudged crystal of my monocle
I realized without reservation
That I was in not only the wrong time zone, but the wrong time
The whole business made no sense to me as I crept back into the void
To try to get back to a sense of order
And far away from "influencers"
(whatever that means)
To hop the wormhole back to my turn of the century town house in foggy old London town
To the warmth of fowl, fish, pheasant, black pudding, savory pies, with pastries and jellies for dessert
And a crackling fire and
My pipe
My pipe
My pipe

John Cusimano

TOO MANY BOATS

Too many boats all up in my grill
Too many boats ruin my view
I sit here in Malibu
With a previously unobstructed view
Of an off shore drilling rig or two
Or three or four, I haven't a clue
But the sand is itchy and the water is blue
And I've got nothing to do
Except stare at boats, instead of drills

Tate Donovan

I'd like to say yes
to every green moment.

to get every rebound
and dish it out for the 3.
I want you to win every time cause
with you, I'm just a blind ol' referee

I'd like to get all your stories
and never be on my phone
so go ahead and stall tonight, I mean it.
i'm here till you're all filled and grown

I'd like to say yes
to every green moment

where it's tender and new.
we're entering this together
and I couldn't be happier it's with
you.

Tate Donovan

I'll have passed
that day on the calendar many times.
'Course we know not the hour
But I hope it's in April.

Not just cause it's the cruelest month
but, I'd like my wife
to walk out of the service and squint
from the sunlight
and feel the same breeze
that moves the Redbud trees.

It might mean something to her
that the honey bees are busy again
and the traffic lights still work.

Spring carelessly begins again
and again and she'll think of me until,
like a November leaf,
it's her day of the year
to let go.

Tate Donovan

Our Father, who art
in a place you can't get
to from here,
Hallowed be thy name.

I gotta remember I'm gonna
die one day
when the gas runs out
On this Eternal Flame

Thy will be done
on Earth as it is in Heaven
How many times do I have
to learn that god dam lesson?

We get our daily bread
every 12 hours,
trespass like teenagers and
never know forgiveness

But please Lord, send me
a temptation
Anything, to get away from
this stillness

Tate Donovan

THE BARKEEP

Working behind that old wooden bar
felt like lookin in a stolen mirror.
It all appears the same,
but what you did wrong
after time gets clearer.

I poured Eamon another double
and chuckled as he wobbled on out
He was young, lonely and loved 3 things:
His Ma back in Ireland, chatting and stout.

I'll never forget the cabbie's tear stained face, or the way poor
Eamon's bloody body did lie,
But the thing that gets me, was how i teased him,
and talked'm out
of getting dry.

We do awful things without knowing,
and won't let ourselves think
But young Eamon's death, just 27,
haunts me with each and every drink

Tate Donovan

There beside our fresh smelling house,
laid a newly washed, floral blouse.
I ventured out to take a look
and saw our pup, avec sock, who gave it a shook.

I chased him about, cursing the naughty four legged cur,
but he dodged me left, faked me right
and appeared to his master
as but a blur.

Pretending to have, betwixt my finger
a piece of meat, in hopes he'd linger
He slowly came, nose in the air
and dropped the now dirty footwear.

I picked it up, victorious!.. along with the blouse
but the door locked behind me
and we could only peer inside
 the empty house.

We sat there together, the clothes, the dog and I
perplexed and bewildered at what went awry.
He licked my face, I said 'good boy'
I texted my wife and hoped not to annoy

I failed at laundry,
the dog was a lout
but we waited together....
which I fear, is what it's all about.

Jodi Egerton

And you're pulling me down the street again
We'll tumble through the city
Pick subway stops at random
Who knows what could happen
We've swapped dresses today

If you get a good fortune, you have to eat it. You just have to.

And you're pulling me down the street again
Your stride so insistent, each step propelling us both
Another corner cafe
Where we huddle over steaming mugs
Earl grey, milky, always

When I picture your arms, they're covered in art, but they weren't, not yet

And you're pulling me down the street again
My feet stumble, trying to keep up
We stalk the stage door of the Fantasticks, again
Snow flurries swirl on our stolen bought shoes

It's always midwinter on Sullivan Street

Jodi Egerton

Breaths of brine
Crisp sunshine
Ink on the ribbon
Verbs fly

Blowtorch on the rind
Smoke in the glass
Ice tames the fire
But the bite's still fierce

Rose petals unfurl
Layers unwind
Velvet and musk
Dance on my smile

The smudge of newsprint
Marks you as mine
Though dawn hits early
Thumbprints shine

Jodi Egerton

FOR EMILY, WHENEVER I MAY FIND HER

You did not take no
But there was nothing left to take.
A fierce, thick night within a night.
Copper lightning streaming out of your chewed-up fingertips.

The massive shop doors slid along metal rails.
You slammed against them and I glanced down at the tennis courts,
To see to how everyone was handling your rage.
But the sound didn't travel.

It was just you, unraveling,
And me, gathering up the threads,
Pressing together the shreds and shards.

We'll piece it back tomorrow.
The weavers will send us away.
We'll hammer our names into silver.

The ink of the printing press
The milk in my tea
The spinning clay
The molten glass

The clowns are moving benches.
Noses 'round our necks.
Torpor.

Jodi Egerton

I've run out of letters and the ones I've got can't cram together right to make you

(one chunk of lip jagged where the dog bit)

I'm shredding words and clay and these stupid waxy crayons and trying just to leap beyond time

(Gray's Papaya, scavenged trees, slushpuddle boots, and you, mid-stride, outlined against the skyline)

Breathe you back, breathe you right back out of the ink and pulp.

(the rain is here. it's time to tech. dayenu)

Jodi Egerton

when the dog took that bite
out of your upper lip,
your dad sat with you in the ER
and you were five and you were scared
and the nurse gave you
a rubber glove full of ice,
a hand to hold against the bleeding

and then it was 93, the all-women summer
and you'd planned to get it fixed,
sand down the old scars
and waken fresh new baby skin beneath

but you didn't.
decided to let your lip be,
though you left me for two whole days,
and two summer days was eternity

and eternity seemed long,
but it turns out that
eternity is longer.

Owen Egerton

Dad says it's bird crap.
But I know better.
It's the snow that never melts.

Owen Egerton

I am dark meat
I am goat milk
I am yogurt with no fat
I am Betamax
I am Zest soap
I am Porky's II and III
I am middle toe
I am back tooth
I am hairs upon the neck
I am real cheese flavor, powdered milk, coffee flavor crystals, Delaware, Pine-Sol, Dig Dug, Joni Loves Chachi, beige cars, plastic
shoes, pounds and pounds of lukewarm pasta
I am F bomb
I am v-a-g-i-n-a
I am DON'T CROSS
I am STILL LOADING
I am GRATUITY ALREADY ADDED
I am still life
I am mid-life
I am life with parole in seven
I am nylon, white-out, perforated cardboard, canned eggs, sweat pants,
Magic Cards, Manimal, poison oak, guppies, Notts Farm, hard sell, soup
cracker, air freshener, peach floss, puppet eyes, a million swaths of
Home Depot house paints and the one hush puppy left in the discarded
Long John Silver take-out sack.
I am.
And I shine so bright I'll burn your fucking eyes out.

Owen Egerton

I'd pay you
for sex.
Could be fun.
You'll take my cash
I'll do this for this. For this I'll let you do this.
The haggle, the hour of an owning illusion.
Feeling, she's nothing but mine till the clock chimes.
Would you pause and whisper Do you want this, too?
And when I nod breathless
You smile,
That will cost you extra.
And I'd know who was leading this exchange,
How my wanting insures your power.
How you are never nothing but mine.
Still.
I'd pay to touch you. To watch you. To be in the room with you.
I have no way to pay.
I have nothing you do not have.
We share a back account, for godsake. We share a bent house.
We share thread-thin credit cards and children.
I have nothing you need.
So I offer it all, everything I am and will be,
all in exchange for an hour or day of you.
And maybe you'll agree.
Maybe you'll smile and throw in this as well, on the house.
(On the bent house we share.)
And you'll smile.
And I'll know
that even for the highest price,
your giving pays my endless debt.

Owen Egerton

I'm terrified
of the cancer
the choke
the car crossing the line
the brain bruise
the trip, bump, black
Terrified
Two days ago I swam in Barton Springs as a soundless lightning lit the pre-dawn dark.
"Ever seen lightning hit the water?" he asks. "Makes it boil. "
A nice way to go, I think, if you have to go. And you do have to go.
How can the most elemental fact of life be terrifying?
How can I care about how they find me? Why is it so shameful to die?
I wish this poem had an ending, a landing, a culmination.
But it will end when I stop typing and no one will be the wiser for it.
There's got to be more to it than that.
Terrifying.

Owen Egerton

To say it cheapens it,
    we know.

It's spray painting the word white on a new white wall
    or love on the forehead of a newborn.
    or shouting in that dark center of night,
    BOY, THIS SILENCE IS EXQUISITE.

To say it cheapens it,
    we know.

Stories help,
    saying something by saying something else,
    feeling the fire best from the corner of our eye.

Still, to try and say it at all
    is some kind of sin.
    A tempting one.
    Perhaps irresistible.

All the art of all the world
    is nothing more
    than the collected sin of a people
    who should just shut up.

But if we did,
    what would I do for a living?

Fonda Fisher

AT THE END OF THE SEA

I am laying here
at the edge of the continent
I am at the beginning
and at the end of the sea
Little waves lap at me
Push and pull me
Just like the moon
I sink into the sand
Just a little bit
I am underground
and above it
I am underwater
and floating on it
I am salty
the sun burns sweet
and the ocean sings songs about rain
and I am everything
all at once

Fonda Fisher

BRING CLOUDS

If you feel like loving me
please bring clouds built for two,
tethered to belt loops
and that will sprinkle rain
that will shoot me
full of beautiful holes

Fonda Fisher

GUILLOTINE

this finely honed and
chosen word
nips at my heels
like a
tiny little guillotine

Fonda Fisher

THE ITCH

Along the town of Nescient
where it's always slightly overcast
the goddess Epiphany
files her fingernails
as she floats
in the River Knowledge
neither up
nor down stream
free of its mighty currents
and tides

The townspeople think that Bliss
lay just to the north of Her
in an inaccessible place
like the itch in the place
that's impossible to reach
somewhere so deep inside
or so far away
that gravity keeps them from it
and if they could fly or
even float
maybe they could touch it

But what they don't know
is that
Bliss trails behind her
in little bits

a flotilla of ahhhs
which comes from the light
of their relief
from her sweet scratch

for the itch
they didn't even know they had

Fonda Fisher

THROUGH THE FLAMES

Through this life I will hold you
Through the flames I will douse you
In these things I will bear you
In these moments I will count you
Out of the corner of my ear I will hear you
Out of nowhere I will stand there
Under these skies I will see you
Under my breath I will speak you

Mark Grochowski

DISCONTINUED BEAUTY

they had discontinued beauty
and substituted it with mediocrity
praise be the weak
for they shall disparage the mirth

all your spreadsheets and slideshows are useless
against the marauding armies of the stupid
they're gonna need some elitists for the fire
and some uppities for the spit

ask not what your country can do for you
seriously, we're just about tapped out

* Wow, eerie how things have progressed (devolved?) in the 11 years
since this was written. I am Nostradamus!

Mark Grochowski

HOLD STILL

harder to handle
tougher to hold
still you bask in her moonlight
and suffer the cold

you swivel her moods like a weathervane
stainless steel smothered in rust
you are the queen's favorite footstool
she is wicked, strong and just

* Dating, myright?

Mark Grochowski

TO LOVE FOR SAVING ME

to love for saving me
from having to finish up that fort made of empty pizza boxes
and Häagen-Daz containers
for making me shower
and change out of pajamas
and groom myself every once in a while

i still cry during romantic comedies
even though i know somehow, just maybe
it will all work itself out in the end

the flash of your lighthouse
spins rhythmically across my eyes
and gives me solace in the ensuing haze

* Ain't (I know it ain't a word) love grand?

Mark Grochowski

NIGHTMARE RADIO

in my nightmare, radio static crackles
like grease on a frying pan
resuscitating compressions and open mouth kisses won't help
i'm dying man

with a wave of your wand
my fortunes would switch
i once could tell wicked from good
and which witch was which

* This is my favorite poem, because I thought I was extra clever with
the Wizard of Oz reference(s) in regards to which witch.

Mark Grochowski

ONCE UPON A TIME

once upon a time
before there was rhyme
and reason was in season

i thought you were mine
i thought you were fine
i must've been blind

but now i can see
that i am a tree
and you are the air
oh what a pair

because without you i'm nothing
a bear without stuffing
a blink of an eye
as i try
to forget and forgive

my heart is a kitten
a lost sock and mitten
a memory that won't be ignored

here again as i start
believing is art
logic will break
your heart

* Thanks to Spoon and The Stills for unknowingly letting me "borrow" some lyrics

Jason Z Guest

CANDIED CORAL CRUSH

Pink and orange sands blend, holding hands in rows.
And days of kissing upon baby blues
return to carefree nights of tumbling shows.
Seven miles of rose and sun dust wakefully blush,
tucking eyes away from ships at bay whose
voyeurs take to land for quick peek-and-plays.
But we, who rest to the slow beat of hearts favor
the Cayman glow of a candied coral crush.

Jason Z Guest

CHANNEL HATE

I spy an evil that screams "Watch me!" in the night,
This monster, so difficult to see,
Its left and right halves dance by strings held tight,
I spy an evil that screams "Watch me!" in the night,
Put coins into its neck, so that it may spit and fight,
Shame on us for grinding to its glee,
I spy an evil that screams "Watch me!" in the night,
This monster, so difficult to see?

Jason Z Guest

CROSSING THE LINE

One pint of Old Charter.
Half-pint of Peppermint Schnapps.
A case of Miller Genuine Draft.
Two things of those Bartles & Jaymes berry-flavored wine coolers.
That was a typical order.
The second our wheels crossed the Red River
we'd hang a hard right,
drop onto his gravel road,
walk into a double-wide
and step up to the counter at Bob's liquor store
feeling ten feet tall and bulletproof –
all wound up on some Nugent or War
coming in off the back of static out of Dallas on Q102.
That old man in Dickies overalls always took our money,
and we always walked out a champ.

I may have only been fifteen years old,
but I was sixteen miles from Oklahoma.

Jason Z Guest

MORE TIME

Through the doorway,
laughter flees the shelter beneath my desk.
Toting sweet giggles of shine
Little plump legs spin,
swishing
away in allegro time.

Ages later
the footfalls chase fur and bouncing ball.
"Look, Daddy!" they chime,
an innocent clamor I welcome,
developing
through the doorway of mine.

Through the doorway
in protests of beet-red sweat,
weighted backpacks sign
of a fleeting youth standing tall,
sprouting
like the trellised vine.

Now, with a foundation
in truth and reverence sown,
for more of every moment, I pine.
Two precious gifts enter this world,
departing
through the doorway of mine.

Jason Z Guest

THE HEIR

The old man rests in the corner of my childhood –
he worked inside a little box
with cinder blocks stepping up into his lair.
Like the parrot of the proprietor,
air conditioning
drew in every patron
for a small fare;
his driving range, a place
where the swelter fed the glower,
dressing patrons with dirt-baked ankles
and scorching any neck
left bare.

A few teeth held up his jolly smile.
Behind horned-rim glasses
Eyes and brow taunted you to step in
where a matinee replayed his yesteryear.
Like a hustler closing the big deal,
this grinder
had teed it up with the best
to gallery cheer.
across the road

And it was the game that brought us together –
four quarters for fifty balls
with pastures left and right to swallow my err.
Like a beat-stick of the gentlemanly kind,
my flesh
twisted from the hammering,
torn and bare;
his teachings, a truth,
where I mirrored a groove,
puppeteered shots with fades and draws,

and became the keeper of his knowledge –
an heir:
that until it is perfect, try, again and again,
for golf, like life, is not fair.

Chris Hannigan

GOOD FOR THE SOUL

what you do is
tear off a big piece
of sour dough and
dunk it in some homemade
soup and as you're chewing
you take a moment
to stare out the window
to see the rain fall down
the glass like tears
and realize you're part
of it all and playing your
part the best you can
and that just doing that
is good enough
at least
for me

Chris Hannigan

MY HOME OF LOVE

my home
of love
sits near
the graveyard
where bodies
buried rot
and bugs
hungry feed

I sit alone
in a lawnchair
with a red cup
wait for rain
and read

hearing humming
of half-remembered
melodies

the dirt
holds on
and patience
waits while
clouds gather
dust and filter
light into misty
beams

hearing humming
of half-remembered
melodies

she has broken the form
as a doctor breaks a bone

for the good of the song
for newer shades
and fresh-cut tones

Chris Hannigan

THE THIEF IN ME

I cleared up the trouble
with a mask
melodic words and
some subtle
finger gymnastics

sent symbolic
audible signals
ringing through
a humid afternoon

they emptied
their cashfilled
pockets
emphasizing
appreciation

and I left
hours later
with a crooked grin
and a few jacksons

Chris Hannigan

WITHIN MILES

within miles
the road gives way
to greening paths
swaths of flowerbloom
and daylight stellarsun

we took shelter
under oldgrowth
hemlock and felt
the sudden heartshift
from downsullen
to up and overjoyed

Chris Hannigan

WHO KNOWS?

on the day i visited stone henge
we walked around the giants
the morning after a full moon

i picked up a slip of folded paper
flapping in the tall grass

it had verse scribbled
and inked in a language
i didn't understand

who wrote this poem
what did it say
what would it sound like to
speak the words and who
was meant to hear it

my companion grabbed my
other hand as if to say let's go

the breeze kicked up a bit
and i let the poem fly like a feather
catching the summer wind,
lit and glittering in the light
of the rising sun

Billy Harvey

ACROSS THE ROAD

i drove across the road
lengthwise
it took me
3 hours and 52 minutes
it could have taken
2.7 seconds
*why do I always make things
so difficult*

Billy Harvey

GENE WILDER

my theory is simple
If you are wearing
an old worn pair
of flannel pajamas
maybe with horses
printed on them

and

you find yourself
sitting
on the lap of
gene wilder

and

he is telling you
a bedtime story
that
he is making up
off the top
    of his head

then

you
    my friend
        are in heaven

Billy Harvey

HOME

you think you can
go
home

they say you can't
but

you think you can

and when you do
it's
never

for the reason
you want it

to be

Billy Harvey

PIROUETTE

she crackles and hums
legs like sparklers
her chalky laugh
to decorate 1000 cakes

*you must believe
that i know nothing*

of love

when you see us together

me--a pair of shoulder pads
her--a pirouette

*you must believe
that i know nothing*

as i tumble forward
with the dexterity
of a baby elephant
knowing nothing yet

*and yes
eventually
i will never forget*

but right now
with my clumsy dance
along side her pirouette
she is all that i know

*even though
i know nothing yet*

Billy Harvey

THE ONLY ONE

I thought I was
the only
one,
and then I realized

we all are

Margaret Heltzel

3/4'S FINISHED

It was not a dream
It was clear as the stars in a moonless Kentucky sky
It was 3/4's finished til a bruised sunrise
It was sweet as gold veins drawn on grasp-less hands   It was a
sunbaked nap to halt all plans
It was the stuff of dreams that reality marvels
It was the gleaming thread as the spool unravels
It was safe in the womb of warm waters
now treading feverishly as security falters

Margaret Heltzel

ALL THE DIFFERENCE

Chiming voices and shimmering eyes
brighten the blackness of a moonless night
More so than the string of lights
that glows softly behind us
In this rare event of socialization
I beg myself to say aloud
Isn't this nice
Isn't this something like normal
The sweet sounds of familiarity
dancing upon my rigid shoulders
inviting my own dance
my own try at the light tongued talk
Yet my own tongue holds taut
strung to the grooves of my gaping mouth
Not even a smile can escape
from behind the precautionary cloth
a burden and a blessing
when masked words are bound
by more than four ply fabric
Avert looks speak novels
when eyes make all the difference

Margaret Heltzel

I WOULD BE LOST

Bound to a resolute frame,
a boulder of being
that rolls for no one, no thing
I would be lost
in a river of dampened dreams
wearied by swimming upstream
If not for the made up mind
of a once wandering friend
since rooted in fallow ground

Margaret Heltzel

THIS COLLECTION OF JUNK

The left side of his driveway, guided by the rock wall he stacked in 1962, narrows at the mouth like the old man's at the news of another stone corner cracked by a seemingly blind backerupper, the wall does not lunge at bumpers, so he swears, and he shouts Slovak obscenities, while the old woman, graceful and wise, rolls her eyes, begging, Chuck, please, sixty odd years of similar exchanges dubbed the pair Sweet Heat, Brown Sugar, beacon of light for souls blown sideways by fiery squalls of the Heat, so he retreats to his cave to collect his rage, taking inventory, meanwhile:
Few dozen ball jars in assorted sizes, butter beans, spare coffee pots, twelve to fifteen kerosene lanterns (one, he notes, once rode on a carriage), ancient nail pulling apparatus, enough scrap wood to rebuild the house twice, empty JIF jars labeled minnows in sharpie on half-stuck scotch tape, wrenches/drivers/pliers floating in formation, petite cauldron of lead, hooks and lines, mounted antlers, unmounted antlers, cardboard scratched with notes dated 1997, Len jedno je potrebné published in 1907, etc., etc.
This collection of junk that breeds in the shadows cast by Carnegie beams, that cools a man made of molten steel enough, at least, to rejoin his Sweet

Margaret Heltzel

WHEN LOVE BEGINS

Aglow with burning desire and embarrassment that
could not be cooled by the steady showers of summer rain
the same rain that muffled heart cry
that washed away the single tear shed
from the sloping cheek turned towards the all seeing sky
the sky that watched as vulnerability hardened to shame and fear
distracted shame and humility laughed at fear and need urged
humility to act
and all of the complexities of what if and should not are forgiven
by graces and good natured hopes
when love begins
rain is no longer counted on to
curtain the likes of desire
it is there
it is whole
it is an overwhelming vision of beauty
that begs to be trusted in blindness
and navigated despite the cavernous darkness within the depths
of two aching hearts

Bruce Hughes

DANCING WITH SWANELLE

there was hardly a time he wouldn't remember
his dreams remembered his dreams
the oak leaf in spattered sunlight one crisp sunday morning
that doorway in Glasgow
that hangover in Monterrey
the snowfall of 86 and the car wrecks
dancing with Swanelle, who's sister hated him
3 AM on a misty city street, 6 AM creeping quietly in the front
door, only to discover fire
babies and crying, kids and laughing, stock cars and whiskey
yelling
the dry gulch of a north Texas woman's imagination
and the rattle of promise in the distance
barely a pulse under the surface
almost at once the white noise of time was wiped away
an avalanche

Bruce Hughes

FERAL

there, and there,
angry jagged edges
if she was talkin that day
mostly she'd hum
grab the skin
press it together just right
push through the needle
again and again
pull the thread tight
like a mail order gown
keep the light organs
all tucked up inside
keep it clean while you whistle
keep the animals out
this ones a fighter
I can tell by its mouth

Bruce Hughes

HOW THE ELEGANT FOWL LOST ITS DESIRE TO SING

like old men do
the ones remaining
an undertow of reminding
the record setting fiction
misremembered action
and disintegration
a luxurious world of remorse code
the paradise they speak of
when they conjure up an afterlife
that's the tea time Houdini
and the cocktail hour Hemingway
and the after dinner Ali
all together sitting at the end of the pier
watching shadows bloom
under stone mirror water

waiting for a tug
on the line or some
other bullshit to happen
sour drinks in hand
time stretching out
daybreak to nightfall
a mountain of clouds
so close you can
taste the rain

Bruce Hughes

MOON STUFF

this morning my kid asked me if he was still not allowed to say
what the fuck
depends, really
there's situational gravity afoot
they need to stop with all the moon stuff, stirring shit up
that's what's making the weather funny
they need to stop flying around up there
it's unnatural
I mean, it hasn't been this hot since I can't remember
caution is necessary
I understand the temptation
imaginary arguments illuminate the urgent questions of today
and prepare us for tomorrow
maybe extinct species went out of fashion
as a living creature with consciousness
my biggest fear is getting a lobotomy
sometimes they don't know what else to do

Lauren Jahnke

After summer's glittery gold
Comes fall's fading coppery light
After winter's silvery frost
Comes the spring's rebirth and delight
My life would be different without
The seasons to measure my time
These cycles provide subtle soundtracks
For memories mundane and sublime

Lauren Jahnke

Dirty and begging on the streets
Turning tricks between the sheets
Desperate for some food or drink
Lots of lives lived on the brink
High up in the shining tower
Wealthy people wielding power
Whose interests do they have at heart
Their own or do others play a part
All are a life you have lived before
Who's to say whose life's worth more
Wisdom comes from unexpected places
And from those without social graces
Life is best lived if you have love
Giving you hope to rise above
Life's aches and pains and toils and troubles
A small reward for all your struggles

Lauren Jahnke

On an ordinary night just like tonight
The aliens landed in a field outside of town
The townsfolk saw the bright colorful lights
But didn't know what to make of it at first
If the aliens looked like you and me
There might not have been a problem
But when someone is green they tend to arouse suspicion
No one knew why the aliens were green
Speculation was that they photosynthesized like a tree
Even if they weren't hungry carnivores, they were still demanding and disagreeable
And spoke their language slowly and loudly as if that would help humans understand
The only good thing about their arrival was that
Humans being human, humanity soon stopped fighting each other
And turned on the unfortunate green people
No wonder Earth is near the bottom of the universal list of vacation spots

Lauren Jahnke

The fairies always visit other people's gardens, she thought
Blooming and green and fragrant with smug little flowers
Mocking the thorny weeds and dried plants in her own garden
Why wouldn't the fairies like the other gardens better
She could hardly blame them, she thought
Fairies, butterflies, bees, all the magical creatures
Flitting and frolicking in other people's sunlit gardens
While hers sat dark and neglected and withered like her soul

Guy Juke

A POETRY MACHINE

grey areas mock the shadow of a poet's untended shame
so at once deny thou endureth love's permanence to any
which among thine twin selves serves only to confound
grant, in richest fancy, thou art beloved of so many,
but that your eager flesh none lovest, proves more evident
in truth's absence, disrobing a verdict of innocence
so possessed, sleeping blameless with a murderous tease
plucking distressed bones from a treadmill of loss
whereas enchanted verse doth only fuel hope's death knell
thus likened to a muse's self defeating poetry machine
dispatching the breathy slang of accountability withheld
whilst idle slaves spill the late tears of resignation
cautiously remiss before a promising sea of change
in so purging the surrendered heart's broken treaty
ignorance compromising a zealous storm of hollow substance
as coincidence doth engage heir and executor inseparable
in triumphant union betwixt love's available remains

Guy Juke

DISTURBING THE DUST

THE PUZZLE: Am I dying, in finality's immutable sense of the word,
or just doing time like anyone else imprisoned by so indefinable a humanity.
It may depend on how fluid or shaky your hand is when connecting the dots.
If you chose a straightedge as the guideline, you're condemning yourself
to the monotony of bottomless perfection and creative underachievement;
while blindly resigning the thrill of the chase, or random factor roundup,
to the closest distance between any two event points in the bigger picture.
Time, time, everywhere, and still no time to think or schedule meetings.
Death, though unforeseen, is something we must all be looking forward to.
Young and old alike are tugging desperately at the same short leash.
Numerically organizing every animated cell maintained by a lifelike image.
Simply drawn to the sin of boredom, with all it's sketchy expectations.
The man of leisure still shows up for heaven's saccharin sweet reward,
like some photo image gradually yellowing and curling at it's edges.
THE SOLUTION: A masque of thick lipstick and smoke forge a perfect design
from flawless geometry and/or history's poorly calculated risk factor.
Each of us misdirected by a recurring flash of love, lost then regained

in the course of defeat's preordained hush... the winning-season payoffs.
This reporter's stirring saga, of a broken heart's darkest and coolest ashes,
exposes unrequited loss willfully disturbing the dust of a shallow grave.
Pity they who mercilessly kill themselves in pursuit of the sporting life,
inevitably relocating to the graceful decay of an unaddressed safe house.
Fear dangles the promise of eternal life before a well attended temptation
to cheat death once again, at the expense of a more affordable salvation.

Guy Juke

Floating into a philosophically aloof,
who's who of B-movie crowd personalities.
No need in posing for another term of fire and ash,
too lengthy some years.
This lazy brain, so overfed,
rich with lessons of quiet style and naked truth.
Small wonder there's zero ram
for my 40% halftone gray-madder thinking tool.
This last minute consolation or so,
these dangerous addictive comforts…
these sentimental traits, all too nice to be good for you,
at my age, being oh so wise but stupid and all.
The difference between the young
and among and the dying daze of old-timers
is a dense red crayola map
of the obstructions worked around,
and the game changing interruptions
you resign only chance to get away with.

Guy Juke

REFLEX ERECTION

the knuckles of sweating green bamboo
lend support to swaying sagging muscle tones
like a members only inhumane hunger strike
time stands still as it meticulously prepares
for the much publicized element of surprise
warm breathing on the surface of a whirlpool
the smell and effect of a woman's wet teeth
steaming up a glass wall of gently drifting veils
a mating ritual's tinted window, layers of cognac
softened sheets of hot liquor redeeming misconduct
through the mindful foreplay of inebriation
subdued paint sample shades in a softened peach flesh
stretched over a perfect frame, legs falling apart
she's all bent under and sucked up into herself
crying over the banks of a passing flash flood
her upcoming downfall played out full fathom
a limited engagement, a heart's bankable conflict
"yes and "no" battle it out over a quick "maybe"
resulting in a new improved consumer friendly quicksand
sedated by the warm current of living in denial
resurrected by a much welcomed funerary art deadline
lonely dreamers wake to a loveless reflex erection
beneath passions careless hand eye coordination
draining some poor wanker's upcoming prematurity
"I don't remember,..... why do I do these things?"
dive bombing kiss, kiss, then back away into the drink
deeper into flirtation's spinning wet sink hole
viciously repeating the words "I love you"
then falling down, deep sleeping in the river's bed
passing out before another natural temptation
makes a designing woman's near truth it's own reward

Guy Juke

TOUCHING COMPUTER KEYS:

I still don't know the problem. It's just one of those things you can't really figure out because there are no real instructions. I find a way to work around it all, to solve the problem adequately. I think and think and I just never reach a satisfactory conclusion. One day after another just ticks by and I feel like my rate of production is suddenly slower than a few days before. Like I have lost my power for a while. I always know it is still there, and it will come back. Just touch the right button, the right number of times. Try to sleep off the sobriety, and so I do, but I cheat. The virus is as old as the machine, and I am so used to punching the same buttons, and getting what appear to be results.

I fall into a deeper sleep, where I dream all the trees are black. It is late at night and its suddenly getting cold. I see a shelter on the screen and I slowly advance toward it. It just takes me deeper and deeper into the dream. It is so very dark.... I can't read anything and I can't turn on the light, as if blinded by some powerful urge to create something permanent and beautiful. Something that doesn't have to be seen to be experienced. To be felt. To be truly loved. Spare and drawn simply, then erased back to its bare essence. Devoid of frames and borders. Stripped to its basic core. A thing of natural refinement and almost unbearable beauty.

This fresh new love I feel is so strong it engulfs my senses in a storm of careless abandon, and I fall willingly across the keys. All these keys, repeated in their proper order, as if in accordance with some natural system, governed by absolute truth. The truth is the beauty and the sadness and the endless longing. The aching for love you can only look at but never touch. You can get so close, so close that it seems perfect. A higher definition. A deeper resolution, but it's only an acceptable tolerance level, a focus sharp enough that no one will ever see the imperfection,..... and you're lucky to have ever been that close. Even when you have the intoxicating illusion of achieving it, and everybody suddenly loves you for sharing this amazing gift, for giving tangible form to their dreams for this brief time, it always slips through the keys again. Into the endless abyss of memory, and crying through the same eyes with which we seek these inspired visions.

Some of us are lucky enough to suffer the pure joy of getting it down on paper, or tape, or the computer, but it's still going to pass away. Just like everything else. It isn't beauty until its out of reach, the art is just an imitation of love, and fleeting vision is just that. We haven't captured anything really, except our own egos, and thats not really love. Just like art isn't nature and nature isn't art.

Andrew Long

DEATH SHALL NOT DO US PART

When I go,
buy something
Dollar Store worthy,
a find we'd both
marvel and mock,
small enough to fit
into your pocket
so I can go
where ever
you end up
going.

Andrew Long

LOOK

The mirror
reflects back
whole hideous truth
you try to duck
the little monster
Every time you return
you realize you're
shit out of luck

Andrew Long

NEW MEXICO SUMMER OF '78

It was never like that.
Time erodes the rough
and slicks memory
believing it was all laughter
and togetherness.
Just remember New Mexico
summer of '78
when the car's radiator blew.

She slapped him
still a little drunk
as he was about to lift the hood.
You could barely see over the dash
but I got a good look.

Andrew Long

ONE TWENTY SQUARE

We held on to summer
longer then either one
thought possible, or probable,
considering the situation,
we were for a time the secret
of the light, bounding forth
without anything to stop us.

All else worthy of mention
is dim comparably, though
slipping that mixed cassette
into my pocket as I boarded
the ferry was killer because you
knew I'd play it incessantly for days
balling my eyes out over you.

Now as I look at the high shelf
as that worn Rollieflex peers back
reminding me you're dead
with a roll of film that I cannot
bear to develop lingering inside
of last vestige suspended.

You taught me that, how the light
shapes the silver with alchemic magic,
and it never got old. All those times
I sat on the corner stool watching
you totally lost, unspooling your
latest against the red light
like a teenager devouring a book.

Let me be blunt.
I'd rather let fog take over

obscuring that roll
then fix it permanently
and having to accept
what I cannot control.

It is the same reason I let nature
embrace your gravestone
I need to be with time
as witness one never
ending song playing
the secret of our light.

Andrew Long

ONLY

If there were a way
To evaporate all the water
We could easily divide
The ocean from salt
And begin to cross
Over to one another.

Until then we will fail
And drown down.

Gareth Maguire

A NICE THOUGHT SURE WOULD FEEL GOOD

The sea is old and tired this evening
He isn't in the mood to wave
And when he tries
It is a sad greying resigned sort of wave
And I'm walking in place
At the beach crossroads
Squeaking to black memories
Beneath the sand
A nice thought sure would feel good
The moon mirror on my face
Stops me for a while
To show me a lost man
Regretting his regrets
Trying to remember
Where the sin started
And if it ever ends.

Gareth Maguire

HANGING ON UPSIDE DOWN

The chandelier's new sky
Was the cobweb covered ceiling
Of the antique store
It spent its days hanging on upside down
Dreaming of his past life
Of situations he'd shed light on
The family arguing beneath him
At the dinner table
The young couple plumbing each other
Sideways under his dimmer hue
The seedy barroom
The dingy pool hall
The stint in the strip club
Gazing outside
Reflecting on the rain slicked streets
The casino
The cigar smoke enveloping his body
As he watched thousands of dead dollars
Change hands at the poker table
The 24hr diner
Up and down
On and off
Flipped over and over
Late nights and early mornings
Forgotten as he was left
Burning for days
Weeks
Months
"I've had quite the remarkable existence"
he chirped to the grandfather clock.
"And if there's nothing to be written
Or indeed read, in this next chapter,
Even that in itself will be something."

Gareth Maguire

IN MY HOUSE

I'm still waiting for you
Whoever you are
Nameless
Faceless
Floating on the wind
I love you
But I am afraid to follow you
Afraid the kids will wander off on their own
I'm still waiting for you
Whoever you are
You're late
You're ahead of your time
Ahead of mine
But late
I sit gazing out the window
I watch the night
Wash down from the sky
The moths come out to play
They flutter around the outdoor sconce
Like white confetti
Celebrating the marriage
Of light and night
I cry out for you
Cry out in the dark
Cry out to a place
Beyond love
Beyond hate
Where life and death
Sit holding hands
Waiting to be born
Waiting to die

Gareth Maguire

IN OTHER COUNTRIES

Standing at the edge of nowhere
Moonlit emptiness
Black washing me
And my shadow
The wind of nothing
Whispering to me
In dark silence
Swaddling me in his invisible blanket
Running away from you
As I have run away
From the others
Shouting in a voice
I'm still trying to find
That this is my story
And it will continue
Wherever the end is beginning

Gareth Maguire

STUDENT OF DREAMS

I popped over to mum's for lunch after mass on Sunday.
"Hey mum, how are you?" I asked.
"Good", she said. "How did you hurt your leg son? I noticed you limping on the way up to receive communion."
"I didn't hurt my leg mum and I'm not limping, but thanks for asking."
"Well son, whether you're aware of it or not, you are limping. As a matter of fact you have always walked with a limp, maybe it's just getting worse as you're getting older."
"Really", I replied, "that's the first time anyone's ever mentioned it."
"Well, I'm sure many people have mentioned it sweetheart", she continued, "you probably just didn't hear them. After all you are completely deaf in one ear."
"What?", I said, "I always thought I had perfect hearing."
"Well", she said, "I suppose in relation to your eyesight, your hearing could be considered perfect."
"But mum", I said,"I have 20/20 vision."
"Is that why you have a guide dog lead you everyhwere son?" she said.
"That's not a guide dog mum, that's Lucy, my wife of five years."
"You're not married pet", she said, "as a matter of fact you've never even had a girlfriend, which is hardly surprising given that you have a face that only a mother could love."
"Funny", I said, "I never really thought myself unattractive."
"Well son", she said, "you have never been much of a thinker."
"But mum", I said, "I am a professor of logic."
"Son", she said, "you are a professor of nothing, only a student of dreams, immersed in your books of fantastical reverie, trusting all that you see or seem to be life as you drift through your dream."

Tim McKee

EBB AND FLOW

through the doorway to the Sea
he speaks to Her Majesty
twinkling diamonds blinding
salt and sand reminding
a stirring morning glow
the ocean breathing slow
holding bittersweet goodbyes
green eyes to the horizon

Tim McKee

she whispered low
between thunder claps
i'm on board
burn the maps

a tale of Jackalopes
and the Rio Grande
sage brush
and corduroy sands

twinkle eyed story
mischievous grin
summer rain
shiny skin

the highway cried
the clock let go
so many miles
since New Mexico

Tim McKee

THE GREY

Poised for purpose
The sun is set to wake
In the morning you'll see
The miles you make

You left a letter
All the things I know
About being stuck
But too afraid to show

Silent and slow
The grey gives way
In the morning I'll ask
What does the Heart say?

Tim McKee

THE SWEET

Distance and time pay no mind to the gravity between us.
Such power and pull, these hearts of gold defy all reason.
How the hummingbird always finds the nectar.
Hold Love with an open hand, for you cannot direct Her.
We shall not cage the bird or bottle the sweet.
For what if Love is just feeling your own heartbeat?

Tim McKee

Your chestnut eyes sparkled. Lit up on bubbles.
We danced as the earth shook. Free of troubles.
The broken chandelier was a million shimmering pieces
Under those peep toe pumps and romantic caprices.
It took me back to the Trashy Diva on Royal Street.
How the clock stopped. Frame by frame, beat by beat.
And how you looked up at me in full surrender.
To have and to hold, I'll always remember.

Seth Meeks

CBD

We move through streets
Like mists, like lovers
Who can only love
When incomplete
Alt-incense dreams

Hear the butterfly scream
See the lizard green
lightning lean
Alt-desertly

I can wish it would rain
I can bum another cigarette
Suck it down
Then be sick of all this rain
Right now dusted time
Wears silverfish sleeves
Alt-desertly

Seth Meeks

DENIM SHEETS

Austin heat, denim sheets
I want to roll with you
Baby
Alt-desertly

Be my tumblr weed
Be my weed-smoking mama
Won't you be my need
Won't you be my need
Alt-desertly

Seth Meeks

GRACKLE JACKSON

Lying awake she says
What do you think about
Painting the living room pink

And you always get what you want
Why do you even ask anymore
And you always get what you want
You always could outlast me

But when things are like this
And I'm wracked with the yips
And kisses are bottomless
And the bottom is feelingless

Grackle Jackson
You're a real Grackle Jackson
Grackle doodle doo
That's a real Grackle Jackson move

Seth Meeks

16

I was a horny little hare
with a bunny-long waist
fast eyes and a harp in my cheek
I could pout with the placement
Of my feet
I could jump and touch your ceiling
When I was 16

Seth Meeks

US AGAINST DEATH

Is there a distant year for us
Against death
And not one another
When the saddest story
Is that some sure
Is only just almost
And all the bloody hands
Are the hands of healers
I hope I get there
And find that distant year
And see
Us against the universe
Us against comets
Us against suffering
Us against death
And not against you

Silver, Gold, Home
Seth Meeks

You asked me about my childhood
About the woods
About the time I came upon
That wall of trees
Squeezed in so thick
I couldn't go between them
Tall enough to brush the moon
You always ask, what did I do?
Because you know this part
I called out for you didn't I?
And I called out for you
And you climbed down from the moon
And you found me and licked my hair
Fed me your cold blue chocolate

And spun me up in a hope
About a secret road that leads
Through the wall of trees
To silver, then to gold, then home

The moon's ghost eats everything
There's no magic left
 in her sleep, their rare breath
Cast the cloth across me
And mends my silver eye
Stays my silver bow until
My silver heart is filled

send down on you
shrines of terror, storms of snakes
daggers
you were an army
Of witches, a world-sized threat
cannon with wings

Of death to death I sent you
Along the waist of Satan you went
Lept the pimpled ass of Heaven
And found a fair home
Down some nameless street
In Canada

Felix Morgan

AS NIGHTFALL CAME

A man smells different right before he kisses you
And different again when he's going to leave you
I hunted through your shower like a weird wet werewolf trying
to find out if you had
Changed your soap but it wasn't me that went stale

~

Felix Morgan

FOX AND CROW

Seth and I made ourselves afraid of the moon
Because it could be a giant
Who eats women instead of loving them
Or maybe it's ball of space cockroaches
Around a lid that's sealing
Somewhere darker
Where souls are traded, cold for power

We run from witches and court werewolves, we build robots and castles
That hold back the rain for our
Spindly children
We can spit and bemoan or unabashedly enjoy the worst
Of the golden age of people and television

He plays me songs he likes and I say that's cool
Even when I don't understand what's cool about them, really, and he
Reads my Adam Driver fanfic when that's all I can write
Because the moon won't leave me alone

Best friends is holding the plot threads and the bad days
Standing in the tentacled fog alone and together
There's a soup for any kind of life's pleasure and pain and
We know how to make it for each other
(Or order it online)

Felix Morgan

ICI TOUT EST BON

There's a man at the bar and his cheekbones are crystal origami
Someone treated him badly once and now it's okay
If he treats everyone else carelessly
He breaks the legs off of small glass horses
Girls who went to good schools and thought they had to flatten their hair or their bodies against the battering egos of bulls like him

We were a real horse, once, in a different life
When the earth was more green and more brown
There were giants then and none of the mountains had been sanded down yet by empires or industry

Everything in my house now is soft and beige
I live in bread dough, uncooked ravioli
And that's why I've decided to replace my veins with neon tubes
Instead of glasses I'll wear spells over my eyes
I'll be a yarn bomb, instagram installation, with sharp ironic teeth and ten feet eyelashes.
I'll be a sensation, the taller I can build my ice cream wigs the more I will be able
to hold the glass under my skin that contains
bright pink and yellow anger inside me when
I'll see the hyenas in the polo shirts, snapping at the heels of their latest
projected sexual fantasies

We'll feed them to the meow wolf, the millennials can sell broken shards
to pay their student loans and you'd be worth more
than anything you've made of yourself

let's burn the maps, shatter the hard, folded men.
We can find the bones of the giants and build homes in their ribs
—a place to be happy
where they never could

Felix Morgan

LOVE IN THE TIME OF COVID-19

My last Adam, with a tree over his heart
Washed my hands along with his
it's a privilege to be lost for a while in an empty bar and
The sharp planes of his face and the softness of his smile and his kiss
And he smiles when he kisses me

We can be a narrow armor touching
The only surfaces allowed
And it's only surfaces we present or move shyly in the light
listening
Laying heavy on his bow of a body
for the sounds of triumph or disaster to ring
Through the windows and the newsfeeds
We wait

Felix Morgan

THE MOON AND THE WIND

I lie down in the shadow
Here and here again
The gaps between my mother's words and your father's untimely death
Between a barking laugh and the hushed way
You reach with your thumbs to spread me
I become young, as uncertain as AstroTurf, rootless, enthusiastic
Three seeds, four months, one chin dimple and a loose handful of apocalypse
You've been my summer shade, baby
My dark spoon and each hopeful autumn moon you set like a coin
so gently on my skittish eyes
And I can rest

Michael Natter

3/4'S FINISHED

Music is Magic
But you only have 12 notes
With a plethora of beats
You can make whatever floats your boat
You can make them laugh
You can make them cry
You can answer all their questions
Or leave them asking why
Yeah it's all about timing
And how you turn a phrase
Whatever kind of groove you're in
Like Heart and Soul or Purple Haze
And what's up with that time signature?
3/4, 4/4, 6/8 and more
No, they are not musical fractions
They tell you what kind and how many can dance on the bar floor
I helped write a waltz once
It really changed my life
That 3/4's finished now
So I don't have to write it twice
Yeah, along time ago
I said, "I won't give Up"
And all my dreams came true
Inside my overflowing cup
Inspirations are never ending
If you know where to look
You might find it in your lover's eyes
Or in the sky or in a book
It doesn't matter where it's from
It's all from the same source
Call it God, or call it magic
It's all up to you, of course.

Michael Natter

A BAD WINTER

There once was a boy named Flinter
Who got stepped on an icicle splinter
It went up through his toes
And came out his nose
All in all, it was such a bad winter

Michael Natter

BUGHOUSE

Be yourself
Unless you're someone else
Get to know who you are
How you ask?
Open your heart
Use all the tools you have
Simple?
Everything is... once you start

Michael Natter

SILVER FISH

A small silver fish
Swims in its own little world
As do all of us

Michael Natter

WHAT'S YOUR NAME?

What's your name
I am that I am
Age?
Somewhere between 39 and eternal
Height?
Does it really matter?
Weight?
Why wait?
Sex?
Yes plz
And when asked my religion
I simply answer, Love

Nancy Natter

CHIVALRY IS DEAD

He was dressed to the nines
With his freshly polished wingtips
And his black velveteen jacket
Everything about him looked sharp
Enough for her to give him that look
He's the kind of guy that opens the door for her
Helps her with her jacket
And pulls out her chair for her at the table
This stuff is more of a fantasy these days
I'm lucky to swallow my last bite
Before he calls for the check
And I rarely get my seat belt on
By the time his foot hits the gas pedal
Chivalry today looks more like
Your man shutting off his phone during dinner
Don't get me wrong
I love my man
I just have to stop watching those old movies

Nancy Natter

NIGHT STALKING

Many nights I spend
Walking through the dark
Singing isn't an option
I never want to be discovered
Hiding behind old oak tree trunks
Whenever I see headlights
Or hear the leaves crunch nearby
How many creatures are out here with me
Doing the same thing
Waiting and watching for any movement
Silent stillness is my reward
The hush and rush of cold air
As the moon passes behind a cloud
The neighborhood owl gives a hoot
I am not alone
I am being watched
I shiver and swallow my saliva
Am I being stalked
Do I hear something breathing nearby
I plan my escape
Executing every detail in my mind
Until the moon hides again
Finally it all goes black
I make a beeline for my back door
Pushing it open, I'm safe
It's a jungle out there

Nancy Natter

WALLS

Ancient walls surround my bed
Telling tales inside my head
Plaster peeling making shapes
Illusions that I contemplate
Random forms become my friends
Peering through my mind's sight lens
Beastly bears and birds of prey
Keep morning boredom at bay
There's funny faces and kitty cats
Flying bats and one fat rat
I've spotted sailing ships and elephants
Even pelicans and skeletons
Hearts and darts and flowcharts
Evil eyes and private parts
I even found a horn of plenty
Pouring out the number twenty
There's a buxom babe in a bustier
All covered with beads and lace
I squint a little to make her morph
Into a stogie smoking sailor's face
Oh, the things I see upon these walls
Awake my dreams as eyelids fall
Fast asleep with images galore
Before I can count to forty-four

Nancy Natter

WITH A SMILE

She frowns with a smile
Biting her lip till it bleeds
Her truth uncovered

Nancy Natter

WITH HIS TONGUE

Because he has no lips
He kisses me with his tongue
It's all he really knows
But for me it's not much fun

J.W. Nickles

INTERVIEW WITH ANNA AKHMATOVA

Dead Russians #1

Where were you born?
The Black Sea's crust   black swans   black roses

How did you spend your childhood?
Eleven lonely years   then I became my own companion

What attracted you to poetry?
     All things ephemeral and tangible   almost everything can be lost

What were the colors of St. Petersburg?
     A memory of snow and silver   destroyed by red and black

What was your fame like?
     A crown of raven gloss sainted with starlight   my shawl the *Sancta Camisia*

What was *samizdat*?
Lines written on cigarette paper   recited in unlit doorways

How were you punished?
     They took the ink from my hands   the blood of my heart

What inspired your work?
     Only this   only Russia

Is that all?
     My poems were wounded doves I held close   until time to let them go

J.W. Nickles

INTERVIEW WITH GEORGE BALANCHINE

Dead Russians #2

How did you discover dance?
    A choice of academies   Naval or Ballet
        a flip of the coin and I set sail with the Maryinsky

Where did it take you?
    Away from Tsar-less Russia and its cities drained of music
        Monte Carlo had so many pearls   one could be picky

Why did you choose New York?
    It has an abundance of bricks   like our Civilization
        in between the columns you can see light

Who has inspired you?
    Angels and felines   (Do you like cats, dear?)
        and then Suzanne   my Stradivarius

Why didn't you have children?
    You know   babies look like little Eisenhowers
        Much easier to make a baby   than a proper loaf of bread

What is this ballet about?
    Here are the steps   it is about nothing   it is about Time
        It takes twelve minutes to dance this ballet

How do you create?
Only God creates   I assemble cakes from stolen ingredients
        I write icons on moving bodies   meditations on the Divine

J.W. Nickles

INTERVIEW WITH SOFIA KOVALEVSKAYA

Dead Russians #3

Do you remember your nursery?
    There was a shortage of wallpaper
    rose trellises unwound into scrawls of equations

What attracted you to mathematics?
    Ciphers shimmering like golden keys
        I thought no door could remain locked to me

How were you challenged?
    So many obstacles   barricades of bitter masculinity
        my own father a Golem in the road

What was your breakthrough?
    I calculated the potential of Saturn's rings
        They'd rather I taught arithmetic to schoolgirls

How did you compromise?
    A university education for a marriage of sorrows
        Our daughter was the tear we wept

What was Stockholm like?
    A chair finally extended   made of light and laurels
        The rotation of a solid body about a fixed point

Do you have any regrets?
    Love is a theorem that cannot be proved
        I failed him   but he also failed me

What is your biggest strength?
    Erasers can destroy everything

I embrace the nothing   and start agai

J.W. Nickles

VLADIMIR FOR VERA

In the relaxing chamber
    the humidity hung in strings of pearls
        the wallpaper buckling like her knees
            he adjusted his tie   and waited

through a window the sunlight
    caught the yellow of her head
        the veins pulsing blue against the dusk
            nectar seeped from her mouth

her eyespots blinked open   shut
    he touched then spread the iridescent
        scales too fine to see
            her body prickled only slightly

and he mounted her on fine linen
    taking care not to tear her wings
        as he pinned her there
                pinned her into place

Nina Otazo

BLAME

whenever we meet
we search for a funny thing to say
to break the tension
the connection
the mention
of the past
the beckoning future
the charged present
to put space between us
to wedge the laugh
as a barricade
for the conversation that awaits
that never stands a chance
will never come to pass

Nina Otazo

DEMENTED

the questions are a dead end
the connecting thread disappears
the tapestry of our conversation
the plot is lost
you ask who wrote this poem
I would rather not confuse you
I say you did
it quells the confusion and jealousy
she can take all the credit
she has lost almost everything else

Nina Otazo

EAR TO THE GROUND

You turned off the lights
Nothing more to see
As night descended
Blinded by the lit canopy

Roiling sky of beaming spheres
Jumbled perfection of coiled serenity
Azure tarp swept up in the current
Night for day

Infinite mosaic of vibrance
Forgotten places awakened
Spire sliced through sky and silence
Nestled humanity unaware

Frightening clarity
Inmost strength of the heart
My own fallibility
Potent consolation

Stunning array of bliss
Makes me dream
Losing my mind
In the process

Nina Otazo

QUE SERA

Breaking conventions
Breaking backs
A house of cards
Stopped dead in my tracks

Forged rigidity
Poised to collapse
Aggression contained
Until the inertia snaps

Leaden and flimsy
Braced force can't divert
Sincerely hoping
Someone might get hurt

Nina Otazo

TOSSING IN MY SLEEP

Clouds within turned stormy
Darkness brewing beneath
Buckled by the fury
I just about gave in

Enclosed through clouded sky
Limestone pillow under head
Entranced by descending twilight
I thought of nothing else

Empty of space and time
Cutout of pinpricked velvet
Breath held for too long
I need a miracle

Need breaks its borders
Storm recedes at sunbreak
Warm glow of acceptance
I have been here before

Gregory Page

A TRUE GRAMOPHONE POEM

I'm guilty as charged
For romanticizing the past
When jazz music
Made feet with rhythm move fast
Rewinding the motor
Inside the old gramophone
Dressed in your best
For a dance party at home
The "Hit of the Week"
Would arrive at the post
Your heart skipped a beat with delight
Before cats could swing
Before crooners were king
The dance bands
Were the stars of the night
One hundred years later
A power generator failed
And the city all went berserk
With my neighbors outside
The stars came alive
Because the gramophone
Was the only thing that worked

Gregory Page

ONE HELL OF A SMELL

There are five senses
I once heard it said
There is a sixth
But I can't see people who are dead
With the sense of smell
Straight up your nose goes the air
To the back of your throat
Where you taste what's not there
Like hot apple pie
Cigarettes & perfume
Bacon & eggs
A hospital room
Sweat & cigars
Garlic & gasoline
Halitosis
Old men & Brylcreem
My vision is clear
I just love my taste buds
I have sound in both ears
I like to touch & be touched
The sense of smell makes sense
When it's fresh cut grass in the park
But it's pure nonsense
When ambushed by a fart

Gregory Page

THE OWL & THE SQUIRREL

Once upon a time long ago and far away
There lived in a tree a wise old owl
Whose feathers were all gray
In that tree lived a squirrel
Who was brave as a hawk
One day the owl turned to the squirrel
And said nothing
Because owls don't talk
Together they sat there
Watching the cows below eat hay
Then the owl ate the squirrel
Because an owl is a bird of prey

Gregory Page

THE POTATO EATERS

One evening in April
Over a hundred years ago
At 7 o'clock suddenly nothing happened
But a painting lets us know
Inside a country cottage
An oil lamp is burning bright
Upon the faces around a table
Sits a family of five
In the air the smell of potato steam
Bacon and of smoke
Was a wonderful warm welcome
Filling everybody's nose
They talked about the harvest
And about their guest who was there
Who signed his name with a paintbrush
 On the back of their old wooden chair
An unforgettable moment
Captured so we know
Once five peasants and a painter
Sat together and ate potatoes

Gregory Page

THE TRUE MEANING OF OPTIMISM

Today on the bus I saw an old man
Wearing one shoe that was undone
I said, "Hey pal, you lost one of your shoes?"
He smiled and said, "No, I just found one"

Darren Patnode

AUSTIN 1991

goddamn we were young deb
you were doing fat lines at the hole with your skinny ankles
and we were laughing with the fishermen
(snoopy naked in the big window)
Shiner spilling from the table
you grabbed my balls and whispered i love the dead
and we still fucked that night which is strange I know
now twenty years later your in Alaska
and i listen to reckoning and hope your warm enough

Darren Patnode

darling (my)
if you judy
blume for me
I'll double e
all over your pretty
and we'll make beautiful
henry miller all night
(because we can can)

Darren Patnode

I believe you said ominous
when our bodies were harmonious
(then washed your pussy in the sink)
you went third person when you talked of us
and said the distance between trust
is all the hope i need
a miracle (indeed)
(then we had another drink)

Darren Patnode

YOU AND I HALF HEARTED

if you absolutely had to
you'd find my heart ungaurded
'cuz i have big love for you
too bad we're so retarded

Turk Pipkin

A RIVER DEEP

Alone in a field of green
I came to a river deep, a river wide
with a boatman from the other side who carried me towards the sea.
Left in the shadows of date palms swaying in the breeze, I dreamed I was alone in a land of plenty,
a land of rivers deep and wide, and boatmen from the other side.

But when I awoke my family was pushed in on me.
Nine of us, young and old,
my baby brother born in this strange desert place so far from home,
always hot and always cold
imagining a future impossible to behold,
living a present impossible to change.
forgetting a past that's been rearranged
and dreaming of something rich and strange.

Alone in a field of green
I came to a river deep and wide
and a boatmen from the other side.
Take me to the continent of love, I told him. Wake up, said my sister. You're dreaming again.

The phrase was "a continent of love"

Turk Pipkin

FRAGANTE DELECTI

Bald and round and timid and sweet,
He laid heart and passion at a dear maiden's feet.
To his surprise she said yes,
And his friends were impressed
by the nuptials that led
to their matrimonial bed.
Their life was a game
playful but tame,
till he came home early
and found her quite surly
in flagrante delicti
with a man in a necktie.
Perplexed, he implored gently, like a man still smitten, I thought
I was your magic kitten.

Turk Pipkin

LITTLE MAN

Danny Hope live on the South side of town got nobody but his
Granny around.
One day she find him with a Glock,
locked it and 33 bullets in

her Daddy's old clock.

Granny say, My Lord I surrender up this willful child.
in the summer of 89
I done my best

but this city is riled and burning bright and this wild child ain't
learning right.

How you gonna study, he say,
bullets flying like blackbirds in the night, only fools lying that it's
all right.
No hope, jus dope
and plenty money waiting

at the point of a knife. Right now, right now Is the rest of my
life.

So Granny says,
Who gave you that name child?
Was Granny called you Hope,
change your nappy, wiped your nose and ass. Granny made
them sandwiches
you took to school.
Taught you reading and singing
and praying on ya knees.
Pray the Lord my soul to take
cause we living with rats and fleas.
Was Granny paid the 'lecric bill

When we was about to freeze.
Listen to Granny,
Danny Hope,
O you be dead at seventeen,
yhe saddest, deadest. shiftless chile
I ever seen.
Life begins to happen
when you pull that trigger
on work and love and desperate hope in your brain. Grow up
child. Make it rain.

And that's how Danny Hope
come to see the light.
Come Fall, Danny Hope working two jobs and studying like a
Dean.
Saving for USC,
most determined chile you ever seen.

One night a car pass by
spraying bullets in the rain.
Granny Hope sitting in her rocking chair Caught a bullet in her
brain.
Danny Hope jus walk inside
and get that pistol from the clock.
Tells himself there's justice coming cause of him and his Glock.
Death begin to happen
when you pull that trigger
in your hand.
Let it rain, little man. Let it rain.

Turk Pipkin

THE FIREFLY

It seems so easy to pick
between shadows and light,
But how bright is the light and how trite to believe that you
know wrong from right.
Which is more powerful?
A thousand mushroom clouds that shut out the light Or a single
firefly that illuminates the night?

Turk Pipkin

THIEF OF HEARTS

I am a thief, he told her in the bar, and
I'm going to steal your heart.
She'd never met a Thai man who had blue eyes. She heard truths as he told lies.
My father's a surgeon, and I will be too,
just as soon as my medical school
is through.
I'm going to save lives, one person at a time. Do you mind if I ask, for your hand in mine?

She woke in a white room, a bright light in her eyes, And knew the truths had all been lies.
A knife by his hand, a small cooler at her side. Removing blue contacts, his eyes turned black. Medical school's expensive, he said, that's a fact,

Fifty thousand for a kidney, a hundred for lungs. That's just the start.
I am a thief, he told her, and
I'm going to steal your heart.

Turk Pipkin

TRUE LOVE

My theory is simple
but the proof is complex.
$E = mc$ squared
is only half the story
E squared m squared c squared
And pi are squared too.
No matter how you slice it
or dice it
or vice it,
all of physics, evolution, physical chemistry and my magnetic
attraction to you
is summed up
in this
rhubarb pie.

Try it and you'll travel from the edge of the universe all the way back to the Big Bang.

Ted Roberson

A DUMP LIKE THIS

close to the edge
mos def
broke
af
soft head
the cat, cash, and black
mercedes
lens
out back
diet pepsi
real flat

Ted Roberson

BLACKLUNG SUN

facing you
facing the sun
i had a dream
i held it once
left with the blacklung
left me numb
dark baths and dreams
i let them run

blood river to blue ridge
the peel to the pines
this haunted hotel room
the end of the line
dark baths and dreams
when they flood my nights
i lay with the blacklung
sun in my eyes

Ted Roberson

MY EYES ARE BROKEN SEEDS

i love you like
a mirror
today is good
but, there's also yesterday
and all those pizzas

Ted Roberson

OH, THAT GOAL

lose
drowned
no diffies
cat tracks and flap jacks
it's all in the belly now

Ted Roberson

TOILET

on the campus
of one
as good a place as any
for truth, hope
anything with teeth
to make sense of the pull

Charles Rocha

At the end of the sea
I found plants that needed water
I took care of them
Watched them grow
Their vines gave me fruit
And then my boat drifted
Into you.

Charles Rocha

desperation:
fumbling to open a small baggie
hands shaking, powder baking, mind racing
all alone with my piss

dissatisfaction:
the baggie is empty
im still alone
no longer numb
longing for home

this solution:
standing on the 16th hole
alone on the green
under blue skies
white painted clouds
that remind me of lines
the birds chirp melodies
only for me
now i am sober
now i am free
home is wherever
i happen to be

disillusioned, never
today not for me

Charles Rocha

In The Window
I Saw Us.

Charles Rocha

She asked if i was gay
I said, "No, I'm slant."
She told me to just fuck her.
To which i replied, "Right now, I can't."

He asked if I wrote songs
I mumbled, "I try, but i hate choruses"
He said he liked my verse
I spoke softly, "Don't repeat it."
Write something new.

Charles Rocha

Something
Rich
Something
Strange
Somehow
Witch
Captive
Ate
My
Brains
Poor
Me
Into
A
Dumpster
Strain
Came
Out
The other
Side
With wings

Rey Rocha

And now
And then
And always
We are bound together
For those who wrote this poem
And those who read it
Have mutual obligation
And are bound
Realizing the poem is more
Not about the writer
But to give to the world
Than more to take
The chance in there then lies
For the reader to replicate
The cycle of beauty
That is true art
And the reader inspired
To give more
Than to take

Rey Rocha

Even stars die
They breathe what we are
And that was something
She was entrusting to the gods
It's hard to exact life
So making it exactly feels right
If they have a course
So they, like us
It was difficult for her
Especially when the time came
For her to burn away
She had never felt this way
And that was something
She was entrusting to the gods

Rey Rocha

It was a crime
Or was it?
Stirred an echo
Echoed a feeling
And felt the rage
Of pureness dealt

It's easy to see
Or is it?
Impetus emblazoned
And astral challenge
The room full of blood
Is hard to exact

Did you listen to the echoes?
And have they spun the truth?
The quietude of dawn's bleeding
Is the only thing you never hear

Rey Rocha

It was dark
And it was the moon's objection

In the tranquil
Thank heavens for the beam

Captured completely
Contracting the remorse

I'll believe it when I want to see it
You'll deceive me when it's time

I wasn't walking through the doorway
You weren't leading but you thought

The doorway was a photo
The pictures were only mine

Now the flash has answered vaguely
And the time has spent your wasting

When were you really shouting
And when was I actually listening

Nowhere then and nowhere now

It's only a doorway
And this is just the beginning

Rey Rocha

They were speaking
Quietly they were hoping
Unbelievably, stillness breathing

The sanctity of sleeping
Holding silently, rusted feeling
And the earth spinning
Repeating

Looking down from the ceiling
Of the universe
It was always revealing

This is the way they were
This was them always
Until the time was caught stealing

James Rotondi

in no black science does she ponder the indecipherable
codes of wrinkled text scrawled on the backs of crocodiles
or shared with skinny hands in the mussed cardboard streets
no shelf burst with beezelbub's books pries her sad eyes open
a craned neck or crooked fist never calls her to make her case
in the dim grim hopeless haze I say goodbye to these dour days
she, like the phantoms that sustain her gorged on lesser hearts
marches on calloused feet toward the mountain where lovers die

James Rotondi

"that's what she said"
he said, from bed, tilting his head
as if it was mirth, not dread
that led this petrified Fred
to wrench this misread epithet
from its damn-ed perch of pith
and lay it—writhing and half-dead
at my withered feet, which forthwith bled

James Rotondi

two rock and roll stars fell into a manhole on 5th avenue
plunged through time and the corridors of uncertainty
for eons, yet never lost their aviator sunglasses or jewelry
they emerged on the banks of a lost river on a dark planet
somehow dry and cool and even the hems of their flares
came back crisp and flowing as they trudged across dust
let their hair become bridges across craters and crevasses
and mingled among the celestial stars that greeted them
as members of their own vast fraternity of bright lights
memories that still are invoked in candles and prayers
bubbling wine splashed over gravestones or studio walls
the covers of mad dash magazines in the protean present
and the thin drawers of kitsch shops and hoarder's dens
even their clothing still commands a high, desperate price

James Rotondi

you are not the dead men of the confederacy
and even less the bodies scattered at normandy
neither the ruined spines of buchenwald
or the quotidian collapse in a cancer ward
your death has no such beautiful horror
for you don't even fight your demise
make no stride to outlast or outflank it
but let it live in your house like an honored guest
it speaks to you and you listen, let it run you
the litany of death's augurs do not move you
for he has taken the reins, and jabbed your ribs
watched your dull eyes swoon over nothingness
trapped your spark in a woolen mitt, smothered
the bright-eyed boy with acids, salts and curses.
your dignity will die first; will you even mourn it?

James Rotondi

when the twelve hours is not enough
dust flecks stay and stay, through the rays
or creaks and hems along the rug show up
soft mist gathers in trails within the walls
doorways give up space only to close again
and the footfalls of a lost spirit tickle the ear
then your time as a sage stops, days quicken
purple comes the night's heart on broken wings
damp sounds fill the borders of your hands
and whispers that once stood for secrets
now carry in the cold air a message for angels

Ali Salzmann

BELIEF

We were sitting on the stoop,
waiting for something
to happen,

wanting to believe that
the smoke against the sky
from our Camel lights
could turn us into memory.

Give us oblivion.
Give us red lipstick.
Give us the raven.

We're ready. Give us all
the starry-eyed bullshit
that your worn-out heart
can muster.

Ali Salzmann

GOOD FOR THE SOUL

You said it was good for the soul,
but I wasn't sure how to stay.
I just knew I had to hold
on my shoulders the daylight
and all the misery and happiness
of being someone's mother.

Maybe I was flawed, maybe
I had been burned by the stove
making Spaghetti-Os one too many
times, the tender, wrinkled skin
showing all my downfalls.

Others had been burned, too
and for no less serious offenses—
sometimes at the stake, sometimes
the altar—but does it really matter
how? The narrative remains consistent,

and those of us who haven't died yet
are tired.

Ali Salzmann

HEADED TO EL PASO AT THE END OF THE WORLD

If triumph or defeat were
the only options, I
surely wouldn't be sitting
in this passenger seat
staring at the blue
embroidered hat
on the dash

—or heading into the muffled dawn
where the broken-down school
bus that seems to be leaning
against a live oak
suddenly appears.

The fall and rise of the fog
and curves of the road
give us more questions
than perspective,

but we're learning.
The more we keep moving,
the more the orange dessert
flowers blanket the ground

and bloom from our chests
like hope.

Ali Salzmann

MORNING

We've been through this peaceful reckoning so many times before. I am tired of being awake, alone, eager, staring out at the stone- cracked earth. Haven't I earned the fatback bacon and morning sun swelling over the horizon,   the tea, creamed   honey, and the sound of a gentle, new rain   falling on the roof?

Blu Sanders

DID IT END?

does it end
i wondered as i looked up
as if i met the sky where it was sewn to the ground
oh but it never ends
it needn't reply
for i already knew the answer

Blu Sanders

FACE THE SUN

as we face the sun waiting for the world to burn
the ends of the earth curl up with tips of gray
the mountains all but paper ash
collapsing on our bones of dust
dancing the wind to nowhere
pieces of all of us of everything
floating destinationless
disintegrating infinitely into the infinity
the smallest into the greatest
the meaning into the meaningless
the black into the blacker

Blu Sanders

FAR ABOVE THE WORLD

i imagine you sitting on a cloud
far above the world
kicking up the blue
star dust on your shoes
watching the rippled sky
go out across the globe
that's how i imagine you
far above the world

Blu Sanders

OLD SCARS

we are but old scars under new wounds

Blu Sanders

SET FIRE TO THE STARS

we set fire to the stars
we blew out the sun
we trashed the hotel epsilon
spilled a beer, took a punch a in a fight
when you knocked over a satellite
stumbled out into the asteroid belt
pissed off everyone in astreichelt
when you weren't looking i stole a kiss
to try and upstage the lunar eclipse
light years ahead if we keep up this pace
just two young lovers in outer space

Bob Schneider

EL NEGRO

I'm singing my song
In Spanish

The way it was intended to be sung
In a high falsetto

The girls in the back of the room
Their dresses half hanging off their shoulder

Smoking cigarillos
Calling out my name

In Spanish
The sparks flying off their faces

Their mouths open
As if to catch a fly

Bob Schneider

ITS HARD TO WRITE A GOOD SONG THESE DAYS

My mind was once full of music
And melody and ideas
Now it's a forest of facts
And figures and formulas
I can still remember what it was
Once like…well, sort of
It's only a memory
A city that floats out
Onto the ocean
And is gone
But not quite
Forgotten

Bob Schneider

MAYBE I COULD BE HAPPY

He thought drinking a
Glass of tap water
Alone in his kitchen

Wearing his
I became a lesbian
T-shirt and staring out

The window

Standing in his apartment
Somewhere on top of the earth
Spinning around the sun

At the edge of billions
Of similar stars in a space
Too vast to comprehend

Bob Schneider

STAR SMOKE

You'll smile
And it will be the only
Time you've ever smiled

Your face will
Fall to the floor
With a clang

Waking the stranger
Sleeping beside you
In the car

You'll have a meeting
In a coffee shop in Seattle
Concerning a musical event

That will never take place
The woman you're talking to
Occasionally writing

Down notes with an
Orange Crayola marker
All hope lost

You'll grow much older
And die one afternoon
In a hospital bed

Your son with his heart breaking
Will allow the nurse to discontinue
The life support

And the world
Will spin through

Space forever

Clouds of galaxies
Gathering together
High above

Bob Schneider

THUNDERBALL

Poop head got hairy hands
So hairy they look like gorilla gloves
His favorite band is KISS
He also likes 'Guitar Man' by Bread

Poop head can't get no satisfaction
Takes off his bathrobe
While the ladies watch him
He always smiling though

Poop head like to rape women
He says they want it
But they don't want it
They don't want to be raped

Poop head can't stop
Shooting people with his gun
He got tied up by a lady
And then he died real quick

Poop head eat eggs
He like eggs and he like bacon
Sometimes he sneeze into
A tissue and blood come out

Poop head make tricky plan
With lady with big boobs
To hijack airplane and then
Change his mind at the last minute

Boob lady doesn't like this
She kill poop head but then
Decide not to kill poop head
So he is still alive at this point in the poem

Poop head farts in his pants
Real soft and silent like wolf
But the stink smells up the room
And everyone pretty much knows it was him

Poop head got mad gaming skills
Poop head wears the latest fashions
Poop head can talk in the Spanish language
These are important things to know about poop head

When you speak poop head
Hears click and clack noises
He rape lady and then they love him
Afterwards. He scuba dives sometimes

Boob lady doesn't have a shirt now
She took it off and now it's gone
Forever. She just farts and laughs
All the time with no shirt on

Shit falls out of boob lady's butthole
And it is all over the face of the guy
On the ground. The guy on the ground
Is a stranger and no one knows his name

The stranger asks boob lady for a towel
Her poop is too much for the stranger
He thought the poop play would be fun
But it isn't as much fun as he thought

Poop head is making a phone call
When a hand reaches into the window
And he hits the hand with the phone
Then the alarm goes off

Poop head is raping someone else now
The boob lady is not crazy about it
The pilots are flying over the house

The strangers face stinks real bad

The military men are having a conversation
Poop head seems to have disappeared
No one can figure out where he is
This is where the poem ends

Bob Schneider Sr.

A DARK SUIT

What was the thief wearing?
A dark suit
What did you notice about him?
A dark suit
What was the most important thing you witnessed?
A dark suit!
Is there anything else you want to tell us.?
Yes, whenever I don't know what the fuck to say, I say "A dark suit!!!"

Bob Schneider Sr.

AND SHE WILL

If you have a daughter
Do the best you can
Tell her that you love her
Lead her by your hand

Trust her to be good
Guide her in her ways
Never wish her ill
Enjoy her younger days

When she leaves your home
Let her find her way
Leave the door wide open
She is never far away

Will she come to visit
Will she love me still
I pray she'll always love me
…and she will

Bob Schneider Sr.

IN THE AFTERNOON

In the afternoon
There is no moon
Does that mean
I'll see you soon.
Later on
the light will fade
The sky will be a different shade
The moonlight brings you close to me.
We'll share a kiss beneath a tree
The night will end
I'll take you home
and think of you the whole night long
The next day all I see is you
I fumble through the work I do
But know that in the afternoon
The night with you will be there soon.

Bob Schneider Sr.

INTO THE DISTANCE

Into the distance the golf ball did fly
I'm still on the first tee and wondering why
My golfing is usually not so top fit
I'm wondering have I improved just a bit

So into the distance I looked for my ball
I found it in grass that wasn't too tall
so into the distance I shot it again
It was straight at the green and right at the pin

So into the distance i scamper once more
I knew that a good shot would improve my score
And what did I find, lo and behold
My ball at the bottom of the first golfing hole

So into the distance I let out a cry
"An eagle I shot" I heard no reply
"Go fuck yourself" was the answer I got
But I'll never forget that wonderful shot!

Bob Schneider Sr.

NOTHING WITHOUT END

To have a child and pick a name is not an easy task.
The name you pick he'll have with him
As long as their life lasts
My first child I called "Nothing,"
The second I called "End."
They grew up fast but stayed at home
and they grew up real fast.
The first child was a homebody
The second was his friend
But when the second went away we were
NOTHING WITHOUT "END"!

Jordan Stone

and that made all the difference
which is none
dead is dead
pharaoh or hobo
adventurer or couch potato

Jordan Stone

an instant before
I cum in the toilet   I
 hear my neighbor
fart through the wall

Jordan Stone

announcing your place
is to have your butt in my face
but I like it I don't care
(I'm a chair)

Jordan Stone

I lie down in the shadow
a lazy ninja

Jordan Stone

I say goodbye
but your titties say hello
hello hello

Andrew Swensen

ASSATEAGUE

We think the wisdom of the oyster
Lies in the pearl, glossy and smooth,
But we are mistaken and misguided.
Its wisdom lies in its shell,
And while your thumb may settle
Into the smooth concave echo
Of the pearl on the underside,
Consider the rough-hewn crescent,
A jagged raindrop made from
Layers of time, built from ocean lime
Then timeworn by the tides.
Your fingers sing the praise of
The knobby, misshapen exterior,
Earthen clay, drab, dull, coarse,
Roughly shaped by a child's hand
Then kiln-hardened without polish.
It is good for the soul that God
Made something so layered,
So irregular,
So out of balance,
And called it perfect.

Andrew Swensen

"LIFE AND ALMOST LIFE"

I knew a man who lived his days To get to one from one before; And when he was an old, old man He boasted how he dodged the storm. And I heard the old, old man he'd say, "all that's beautiful drifts away Like the waters. Everything alters." He died and never lived a day.
Oh yes, my friends he dodged the storm. With two sons and an almost wife He almost hurt and almost cried He almost had an almost life.
Not me!
No almost river for me; throw me in the sea. No almost frost for me; chill me to the bone No almost life for me; no almost life but life — All of this life for me, lads, there's my home. Throw me headfirst into the deep! Give me the sun, give me the storm. Give me a bonnie lass and we'll Dance through the night and greet the morn.
I knew a man who lived his days To feed his children and their ma. He turned the earth and sowed his field, And fed them all he did – my da! And I heard my dear old da he'd say, "Don't let the beauty drift away. Like the waters, Everything alters, But find your way to love each day!"
There's Jimmy, Matty, David, you, Then Lauren, Peg, Maureen and Kate; We love you, son, but lords we're not; No pot of gold, nor land for eight."
I knew my dear old da was right For if I stayed my path was set: I'd almost find an almost wife, With almost land, it's almost life.
But no!
I want to live my good, sweet life Make it no less than what I dream. I want to raise a pint to time, And time will raise a pint to me.

Have you ever let the rain fall down your face? Or sunk your hand into the earth? And has the raging wind asked you: Do you live life for all it's worth?
No almost river for me; throw me in the sea. No almost frost for me; chill me to the bone No almost life for me; no almost life but life — All of this life for me, lads, there's my home.

Andrew Swensen

"LOVE IN THE TIME OF CORONA." A SONNET

The longest journey is a hair's breadth distance, The span that crosses from your hand to mine; Though we may be enriched by sacred instants, Impoverished I sit from you confined. I see me pauper and life poor if its Summation measures only meager "I"; The total of my qualities and wits Is momentary dust soon passing by. Since nothing crosses now to mythic there, From fleeting I to the eternal we, I step halfway and wait for you to share The whisper that would be all to me. Unmoved you tautly hold unmoving hand, So leaving I to we a space unspanned.

Andrew Swensen

"THE ART OF FORGETTING"

I wish I could say I was there every moment, Each day and each hour as your story unfolded. Now I'll tell you the truth if you think that you're ready Because one little trick Made sure pain didn't stick: I had mastered a craft, the sweet art of forgetting. In the art of forgetting you paint your world gray, The colors soon fade, the night melts with the day And you see the world as just fog and some mist, And the beast won't find you, Won't be there to remind you, Of your failings and falls, and the weight of your sins.

You think the demon's out there stalking, But that's not where the monster's plotting The beast is born from the darkness you fear, The beast lives deep within, it's in here.

In the art of forgetting, you learn to accept all the colors you miss In the art of forgetting, you quiet all the noise and still all the fits.

I tried to paint the demon inside that held me so tight, So tight as I cried, cried through the night, Now it's time that you know since my sun is soon setting, Each night as I cried, I came to decide To wipe colors away and practice the art of forgetting.

You look for the demon in all the wrong places, You know where it lurks, but don't want to face it. You turn over words, but don't want to say it. It's always beside you, And tries to deny you The chance to forget the self you are hating.

You think the demon's out there stalking, But that's not where the monster's plotting The beast is born from the darkness you fear, The beast lives deep within, it's in here.

In the art of forgetting, you learn to accept all the colors you miss In the art of forgetting, you quiet all the noise and still all the fits.

Andrew Swensen

"THE MONSTER IN THE WALLS"

It's Monday morning at 8:32,
As you start to wonder what's happened to you.
You hide from your husband who's not speaking;
Your head is a fog since your not sleeping
You swear it will change,
Since it's always the same.
It's Monday, every Monday, and what will you do?
You think shelter can build you a shell, Four walls and a bottle to hide you from hell, As you barter with God to stop the drifting, You start to wonder if she's listening...
It's Thursday night at 11:43, And your mirror shows what you don't want to see. The house is so empty that it echoes The shades are drawn on the windows; You swear it will change, But it's always the same. It's Thursday, every Thursday, and you can't break free.
You sought shelter, but now hide in a shell, Four walls and a bottle, your own private hell, So you barter with God to stop the drifting, But soon realize that she's not listening...
It's Sunday morning at 3:51, The monster in the walls has come undone; The growls and the shouts, they ring in your ears, The sounds of your doubts, your 10,000 fears, You swore it would change, But it was always the same, As the monster asks what you've become.
You sought shelter but might die in a shell, Four walls and a bottle, between heaven and hell, So you plead with God as you're drifting, And you hope to hell that she's listening...

Jeff Swensen

after 20,000 days here,
what gets into the blood the deepest is,
that what we thought we got,
we ain't got…
whether we think we deserve it…or not…

there's really no escaping the darkest taste of time,
not here anyway,
the old oaks still fall across the path,
and the coolest waters,
…what ain't been polluted anyway…
still roll through the valleys,
laughing at our clocks…
and if you stop here in Appalachia,
and look down from the bridge,
i'll be that cloud…rolling by…
still reflecting on the water.

Jeff Swensen

After the losing,
I never slept too good.
...and if I did, the dreams
had crows in 'em...
I liked the crows,
but could never make
out what they were
trying to say...
about forgetting.

Jeff Swensen

Here in Appalachia,
there are many rivers,
that roll down hill from all directions,
for their own reasons, never lost...
...but right now,
the mama raccoon in the chicken coop,
at 3 am,
don't seem to care about those rivers,
she just wants to grab a chicken by the neck,
in her teeth, taste the blood, for good measure,
and drag it back to her babies,
sleeping in a hole, far up in a tree somewhere close,
for a springtime thanksgiving feast raccoon-style.
And i would be lost,
thinking about those rivers,
if i didn't have to think about killin' that raccoon,
makin' orphans out of her babies...
so i let her run, with the chicken,
and see that the blood doesn't get lost either,
just rolls on down hill around here,
same as our rivers.

Jeff Swensen

Time talks its tick.
gorging on udders of memory,
while the water in our well,
gazes up from its cell,
and shows us the light
from the deep darkness.

Jeff Swensen

You were snapping out of a wide-awake sleep,
on a plane, above Nebraska, I think...
a trance of sorts,
and mentioned something about being afraid,
that you wouldn't find any place
... to spend your courage.

The lady beside me was sweating the turbulence,
in the palms of her hands,
holding on to the faith,
that she knew there was somebody to be afraid of...
sitting 2 rows up,
reading from a unknown text...
on the uncritical piety,
of a 700-ton hunk of metal
at 35,000 feet.

We watched another dude,
eyeing up someplace to smother a fire,
weighing the options in 200 eyes,
about peace without loneliness...
or maybe,
loneliness without peace?

Luckily they had movies on the plane,
which comforted us back to a poverty of thought,
a wealth of pocket,
and helped me think of something
more than flesh,
every time you exhaled
the pressure.

Jim Walker

10/3/18

You in a new pink tutu,
me with a new swaggy hat,
riding our borrowed bicycles
to and fro, around, up and down
Portland's meandering grid
until
in a park under the trees
that made the northwest
we rest
laying in shaded sun,
giggling forty year olds still
alive
on the far side of our revelations
admiring the untiring gods,
thankful
how they laugh at everything.

Jim Walker

4/10/19

The young pigeon was clearly done for,
a grayish-pink sputtering mess
on a grayish-black driveway,
with a late freeze coming.

If the only life you could save
within your own gray lifetime
was a pigeon, and you would fail,
what value the mercy?

-   surely even pigeons
feel their living and choose their singing
for more than survival, but for a happiness
for as long as they are able -

I repeat to myself to quiet the crunch
memory of the so small skull.

Jim Walker

5/9/19

After the first ancestor in a cave felt a new despair
when the one who cared for her more than the others
did not return with food, did not return at all;

After an old man wrote a love story
of an old man leading his people from danger
so they might receive the laws of the Old Man;

After all the kings' mutual aspiration
to divide the ocean among men
and scribble names on the mountains;

After belief in facts reshaped belief
we live on a sphere on the edge
of a vast and expanding idea;

After history again refused attempts to rewrite
how easily we tended, and still tend, to cruelty
warped in our hand mirrors to reflect as love;

I wake up early and, trying not to wake my son,
step out into the lightening yard as our dog watches
with that way of encouragement only dogs offer,

to take in the morning,
before turning to whatever needs to come next,
just taking all of this morning in.

Jim Walker

6/26/19

I don't remember exactly why we decided to go camping, or why we haven't spoken in years, or if you actually married your grad school girlfriend, or when you moved, or where you are, but every now and then, I come across the photo of you resting against the rock, grinning at the top of Emory Peak with the iconic crooked tree in the background. I remember we had driven to Big Bend on a half-baked mission to chase down our fleeting youth before we fully suppressed those full-baked impulses for half-planned road trips. We sped the whole way of course, with West Texas ever so wider than we could conceive, arriving midday to set camp, slamming beers instead, looking for the trailhead. I remember we only had to glance at each other to decide to go left and up instead of right and back. We almost ran, not even knowing how we would know the end, devouring the uncertainty. At the top, we grinned and rested, spent and overheated, but with our youth briefly reigned in. We took the descent with the same abandon, oblivious to our lack of water and good shoes, making the car at the basin at dusk, crushing more beers. We only had to look at each other to decide to forego camping and drive back to Austin, drunk on the challenge of ill-advised action just because we could still say 'fuck it' and back that shit up. We hit I-10 with a half tank of gas and a turning storm pulsing across the northern horizon like a lit-up cobalt blue sea upended, overtaking us near Sonora with a roiling downpour as we howled at the sky and gas fumes and all the great untold histories we couldn't believe were beginning just now, just here, just before we would never see each other again.

Jim Walker

4/8/20

Down the street, my neighbors and I gather gawking
how the small snapping turtle hovers on huge claws
and glides through the erosion carved pool
under the graffitied culvert. Even a light rain these days
flushes the creek, depositing dark curiosities
from a distant world,
mostly familiar, long-broken things and young turtles,
and we ask ourselves, 'should I do something, or
should I just leave it alone?' After a too-quick minute
everyone disperses, gliding home in the dusk
wondering if the next rain will finally force us
into the world at hand.

Wammo

I FAKED MY OWN LIFE

everyone always tells me
that i faked my life
but it was you
you faked my life
you published Ulysses
before i finished writing it
you released Dark Side Of The Moon
before i finished mixing it
you were performing Howl
at City Lights
before I had even thought of it
you faked my life
you stole my girl
you had my children
you drove my car
you wanted to be me
before i got the chance
that was my screenplay
my sky scraper
my funk band
my brilliant design
i piss Pixar in my sleep
i got chunks of Birth of the Cool in my stool
Jesus built MY hotrod, motherfucker!
i'm Tangled Up In Blue
not you, bitch!
you hear me?
so the next time
i give you change for your donut
you should give me
a little respect
before
i cut you with that
knife you owe me

Wammo

MOTHERWELL

THE MOTHERWELL'S ARRIVED!
THE MOTHERWELL'S ARRIVED!

the other grunt and i
take the large wooden crate
from the delivery guys

BE CAREFUL
FOR GOD'S SAKE
BE CAREFUL!

the art crones
screech jagged
wringing talons

OH MY GOD
THE MOTHERWELL!

drones we are
framers
dressing art with metal
wood and glass
today we are
unpackers

BE CAREFUL YOU FOOLS!

with claw hammer
and crowbar
we begin
our dance disassemble

crate inside crate

foam and wood
and crate again
a russian doll
within doll
within doll

the crones scream instruction
slathered with warning

and yet another crate
and another
smaller
and
smaller
and
smaller
still

a cruel joke
a birthday ruse
smaller
floor littered remnants
and breathing
and tearing
and swearing
until
a frame
placemat size
with a 2 1/2" square
window
cut in the mat board
inside the window
lay
three torn
strips of paper
two gray
one brown

ISN'T IT WONDERFUL!

ISN'T IT AMAZING!
i look at my fellow scrub
at the mess we're going to have to clean up
at the three massively expensive little pieces of paper
and say

Man, we're on the wrong side of the crate.

then I look at the crones
who drilled me mercilessly during
my interview
for this minimum wage summer job
filling my head with
"foot in the door to the art world"
and
"work hard and you might even get your own show"
these crones
whom I pictured impaled on the shards of glass
i pulled out of my fingers daily

i look into their evil
jagged
souls
and say

i quit

i help my buddy
clean up the mess
and go home
to paint

Wammo

RE: MONETIZE

i toured with Lollapalooza
summer of '94
from New Orleans
through Texas
across the desert
up to Seattle
and back down to L.A.
about four gigs into the tour
they barred me from slamming
because i was winning $100
every day

they said it wasn't fair
to the other poets

so i had to figure out
how i was gonna eat
drink beer
coffee up
whatever

i started trading poems
for goods
monetizing my words
performing for
people making gyros
grilling kabobs
serving coffee

the gyro guys were great
every day they'd call out, "WAMMO!"
as i approached
"What have you got for us today, man?"
i'd jump up on the counter

and shout out a poem
over the clatter
the chatter
the music
they always cheered

then they'd make me a gyro
or shawarma
or felafel

at the coffee tent
they'd always try to engage me
in a discussion
about my work
what it means
the imagery

of course, that was usually
first thing in the morning
i was always hungover
and not ready
to analyze anyone's poetry
especially mine

the beer guys were local
in every town
they rarely played along
so most of the booze
came from going back stage
and drinking Green Day's
or The Breeders'
or Nick Cave's

my favorite moment
of the tour
came
when i walked back stage
and there were all three
Beastie Boys

playing basketball
with five
tibetan monks
in orange robes
i sat on a wall
and watched them play
4 on 4
the monks were a lot better
than i expected

i toured
for 6 weeks
with very little cash
living off of my words
and i still dream
of a world
where people listen
instead of
count

Wammo

TEN ROTTEN POEMS ABOUT OMAR SHARIF

1
I can only
achieve erection
when watching "Funny Girl"
Boner pills should be renamed
Viagromar Sharif

2
I shot the Omar Sharif
but I didn't shoot
the debutante

3
Firahs Ramo
loved his mirror
more than his
TV

4
Oh Mar'
Share reef(er)

5
Merve Griffin
had a serious jones
for fisting his guests
after the show.
Up to his elbows
in Carol Channing
and Omar Sharif
he'd scream
"Fuck you, Mike Douglas!"

6

Where's the beef?
Omar Sharif!
Who smokes spliff?
Lee Van Cleef!

7
Once upon a time
there was a little hamster
named Cody
and every day
Cody the Hamster
would skip
into the forest
to buy a sack of grain.
Then he'd drag the grain
back to his sick grandmama
who slept in a tree
overlooking the highest -- Holy Fuck!
It's Omar Sharif!

8
hey Omar Sharif
why is this haiku for you?
Doctor Zhivago!

9
O is for the other films you worked on
M is for the monkey on your back
A is for the arabic you vocalize
R is for your station wagon rack
S is for the slinky way you saunter
H is for the hatred in your soul
A is for the after party's orgy
R is for the riot on your pole
I is for the idiot who wrote this
F is for your shirt in Funny Girl
put them all together they spell
OMAR SHARIF
the thought of you makes me dirl and hurl!

10
Caught between the torrents of lust
for stardom trickles and thins
to flatline in the wake
of shiny newbies
Ask Roy Clark, Chevy Chase,
Omar Sharif, Jimmy Fallon
Axl Rose
They'll tell you

© wammomarsharif 2008

Wammo

UNI

i knew i should have
unplugged the toaster
before prying the bagel out
with a fork

i knew i should have
checked my food for bugs

i knew i should have
put on Otis Redding
instead of Ratt

i knew i should have
poured out that beer
before getting on the highway

i knew i should have
backed away when
the shame cave
looked crusty

i knew i should have
done the watusi
instead of line dance

i knew i should have
read the bible
before the flood

i knew i should have
left the drugs at home

i knew i should have
tempered my temper

i knew i should have
never trusted anyone

i knew i should have
been honest

i knew i should have
moved out earlier

i knew i should have
made tea

i knew i should have
rotated my tires

i knew i should have
paid the phone bill

i knew i should have
made that bass player
audition over the phone
before calling the band

i knew i should have
answered that letter
from Warner Bros.
in a timely fashion

i knew i should have
recorded that song
after writing it

i knew i should have
worn a condom

i knew i should have
double locked the door

i knew i should have
folded

i knew i should have
called

i knew i should have
raised

i knew i should have
apologized

i knew i should have
waited

i knew i should have
ducked

i knew i should have never trusted that crackhead with my unicycle. It's been three weeks now. How the hell am I gonna get some trim without showing off my uni-tricks? It just goes to show you, you gotta plan everything. You gotta be like that ant, not that lazy grasshopper. You gotta keep a grip on things. No one's gonna do things for you. You win some, you lose some. Can't live with 'em, can't lend your unicycle to a drug addict. Boy howdy, if I ever see that son of a bitch again, I'm gonna grab him by his crackhead nose and twist his crackhead neck until rocks fall out his crackhead ears. You hear me out there? You fuckers! You're all against me! I hear you in the next room. You ghosts! You phantoms! Always one step ahead of the game, eh? Well, not this time, brother, let me tell you! I'm saving my lunch money and when I get enough, I'm gonna buy me a bicycle! That's two wheels, fucko! Twice as fast! No one-wheeled crackhead can outrun me and my bicycle and when I catch up to that bastard, I'll get my unicycle back! Then I'll have three wheels! More wheels than you ever dreamed of!

i knew i should have

let it go

i knew i should have
played possum

i knew i should have
watched my back

i knew i should have
picked up
bread
on the way home

i knew i should have
plugged in my phone

i knew i should have
waited to find out
before painting the nursery
pink

i knew i should have
done heroin
on an empty stomach

i knew, i knew

oh whoa i
should have known better

my fucking unicycle

Jared Warren

Dirty Dishes,
Peeling paint,
Couch potatoes,
Late on rent,

Unmowed grass
Piles of clothes
Bearded face
Dominoes

Booty calls and
Late night porn
Blinded dates
Regretful morn (ing)

now with you
we couples mingle
No thoughts of days
When I was single

Jared Warren

If I lie down in the shadow,
And give up on my chance at the sun.
I toss and I turn with my battles,
I might howl at the sky with my tongue.

And the wind turns the darkness to light,
And its absence turns it right back.
But this pile of truth that brings me to you,
Is like the light of the sun in your laugh.

Now and then, when you dip, the light blasts through,
Pierces deep into my soul,
I squint and I dive, keep my eyes on the prize
Your lightness makes my darkness whole

So when I lie down in your shadow,
Your hair partially blocking the light.
The shade on our faces, quickly erases
The hurt and the pain and the fright.

Jared Warren

I plucked a feather from that passing bird
And put it in my cap.
She squawked and squelched a thousand words,
And I could not take a nap.
So I offered up some seed and sugar,
Waited by the door.
The bird took a lick, spilled a bit,
Then squawked at me some more.
And 20 years passed by like this
With sleepless afternoons,
I built a house, a bath, a perch,
And still that noisy tune.
An apology simply would not do,
No gift or sweet sweet treat.
Turns out that feather made all the difference,
A lifetime full of tweets.

Jared Warren

Once in while, I imagine your smile,
As it crosses your face in the dusk.
And now and then, as the dark settles in,
I think of the good and the trust.

So I muster the balls, to reach out and call,
Finding a phone in my hand.
But the darkness reminds, of all the bad times,
So I reconsider the dial again.

The device goes back down, with hardly a sound,
And the memories shift in my head.
Your probably just waiting, while I am belate-ing
The ring to your heart and your bed

But I thought about calling, so stop your bawling,
And you call me, if you you'd like
Or sit there alone, hand on your phone
Like a ninja who can't use a knife.

And there it ends, a night gone again,
With loneliness from fear of a fight.
Soon you'll find a new caller, just as I decide to holler
And I'll regret my hesitation for life

Jared Warren

Without the sky above you
Without the time to love you
Without the brush beside you
And all the time to try to
Find a place to tell you
The secret of what I do
When things inside turn all blue
And wash upon the real true
Things that I must sail through
And things I thought I outgrew
But without further adieu
And life turns into frost
Without you id be lost

Erica Stall Wiggins

AN ISLAND

Tawny scuttle mouse sanctuary
of hay straw and dust motes
dinner is saddle leather and grain

Weathered whistling beacon
smells of silky muzzles and flanks
once crowned with a rooster vane

The vessel takes in the silence
the way the wind measures the weather
and the field waits for rain.

Erica Stall Wiggins

CHRISTMAS CARDS

(Photo: Erica, Dylan, Alex, Nana, and Cali the Chihuahua in Rockport, TX, July 2017)

The holidays are an endless compromise
of garland that quits halfway down the bannister,
wreaths that fall off the door to sit on the porch
wool gift scarves that wanted to be cashmere
even worse, the wretched gift card
that wanted to be SOMETHING.

But the Christmas card,
it's a compulsion,
and it's not happy
until it's perfect
in its non-denominational messaging,
composition of color and photographs
and heartfelt message that even
the niece who lost her child might take comfort in.

Is it wrong to paint a rosy picture?
To leave out the in-school suspension
the ongoing debt,
to omit the head lice?
No one wants to hear about that stuff
at Christmas,
and we did have a hell of a time in Rockport.

Erica Stall Wiggins

FIRST DAY OF SCHOOL

The grey arm of the schoolhouse clock
sweeps the campus clean

the school road is a helter skelter
lot of abandoned minivans
baking on the August blacktop

and those eager kinders
scraped-kneed, soft and small in the bright hallway
still want to be big.

Erica Stall Wiggins

GOODWILL

I took my wedding dress to Goodwill.
It rode in the passenger seat, doubled over but still erect with tulle,
daring all my neighbors to behold its dove-white mass as I drove down my street with it.
It felt less ridiculous to do this than to move it to a new house, and it seemed to be a breath of fresh air to the guy in the donation lane who I handed it to.
I hope that some bride-to-be finds it, and that it's perfect but honestly I don't want to think about it anymore.
At least that's how I feel now, and probably how I'll feel from this day forward, for better or worse.

Erica Stall Wiggins

THE AAA BALL GAME

(Things That Still Happen at Baseball Games Just Like When I Was a Kid, All of Which is Miraculous and Goes on Even Though the State of the World is Kind of a Shit Storm)

Three guys go for the same pop fly, then all stand back as it falls, thinking the other guy called it. Everyone groans.

Someone in the crowd catches an impossible foul ball, everyone cheers, then cheers again when they give it to a kid (can be their kid or ANY kid nearby who is sad they didn't catch it).

Our team hits a home run.

I'm not sure where my kid is for a while, but he's fine, he was just running around with friends.

We leave at the seventh inning, because we're tired and didn't want to sit for an hour in the parking lot to get out. Plus, we got in free anyway because someone gave us tickets while we were in line.

While all of this was happening, the empty house that we call home sat untouched, unbothered, and air conditioned, while our dog waited for our return.

Harold Whit Williams

A FEW LINES FOR THOSE I LOVE

We had a good run, I do declare.
The pomp & circumstantial evidence.
The bomb's earthly delight.

All you can eat. No down-payments.
Bottomless refills. Crotchless panties.
Low fat. No credit. This will

Make your toes curl in pleasure.
Add length and girth.
Fuck you fantasy football.

Shithole country music. Live free
Or diet. That Blue Angels
Flyover cured my Covid.

Harold Whit Williams

MADE FOR TV

I stand tall in the prairie grass,
Final scene of a movie never made.
Smoke signals. Wildfires

On the horizon.
A dove coos one last time.
Lonesome dove.

Last of the Mohicans.
I squat in a clearing, chewing
Mescal beans

To envision all those gods
I created. I hum
The closing credit's theme.

I lie down
In the shadow my life cast.
I would like to thank the academy.

Harold Whit Williams

SAD BALLAD OF ELSEWHERE

This is the dream we all sing
Dead of night. Dead to the world
We all seem to be.
Dead can dance. Dead by August.
This is my call to prayer I snore in C.
This is the verse/chorus/bridge
Of that deep album track
I lost my virility to.
Joy is a blue note, random
And fleeting. Grief is a rhythm section
Always in the pocket.
With a frown we wake to rewrite
Each day's melody.
With a smile we're lowered
Into that rest measure
Beneath the sod.

Harold Whit Williams

SENTIMENTAL HOGWASH

Time with its elasticity –
Such a thing is difficult to comprehend.
So many moons have passed.
Morning, noon, and night.

Like a front porch whittler,
I slice and chip away
At the stob of each day, the same day
– always the same day –

Trying to shape it
Into something recognizable,
Trying to scrape it
Down into some token symbol

Of relevance. But those little tchotchkes
of this moment, of that moment,
All end up simply collecting dust
Upon that sad shelf of the ego.

Harold Whit Williams

SILENT WITNESS

As nightfall came, all the shadows
Melted together
Into one immense funereal shroud.
Birds became skeletons
Perched on bare branches.
Daydreams spun in their little graves.
The TV and the radio
Stopped working,
For which I was grateful. And
On the street next over,
Either a car backfired
Or someone was shot to death.
I said nothing to no one,
Knowing that sooner or later
My time would come.

Chapin Wilson

Chocolate Feathered Mush Bottom was having another bad day
so he made a conscious decision to take it out on the dog.
But the dog was as innocent as she was vicious
and Mush Bottom got all tore up, but good.

Unfond of doctors, he grumbled into another bar and was made fun of
by jokes he respected and would have really liked
if he hadn't been the butt of it all.
But he was, and so, he went cage-free ape shit on the red leather booth he was sitting at
sending foam and springs flying like sewage from a burst pipe.
The bouncers, lurking like hemorrhoids by the exit of the establishment
couldn't help but notice and reward Mush Bottom
with a painful expulsion and bloody violent thrashing under the stars.

Mixing in with the drainage
alone again, he thought
If only I'd done my laundry
I could've started out the day on top. Instead
he pulled up a soft slab of curb to curl around
hugged the concrete and pissed himself
pleased at the warmth, pleased that he didn't care anymore
(again)
poor Mush Bottom fell asleep with only one real regret:
in the morning he would wake up
without a toothbrush
and be unable to feather his chocolate.

Chapin Wilson

In a dream I lost my mouth, like a marionette's loose face drawer
I kicked it down the sidewalk trying to pick it up;
in the dance of the dream it wasn't much prettier,
but at least then they were laughing.

Chapin Wilson

INTRODUCING SHERIFF ALI

I would like to roll a fat spliff
and call it Omar Sharif
fill it up only with kush and keef
wrap it up only in the finest cigar leaf
and chomp it between my teeth.
Then I'd light it up freely, theatrically like a smoke machine for a lift.
I'd emerge intoxicated with levity
from my leisure jet way back in the 1960's
arriving in LA from elegant TWA's JFK
I'd step right off the screen
and clear the smog from the dream
with my very first scene
just a speck on the horizon
deep in the heat of hell
he guards me well
deadly and judicious
full of passion and precision
even on the sun's anvil
he can take the heat
and still smell sweet
David Lean would like you to meet
naturally tanned
fresh, handsome
dark and dashing
but just a little bit shy
my new spliff, Omar Sharif.
Say hi little guy,
High.

Chapin Wilson

there's a nice breeze
between my ears
please don't close the curtains

there was a glacier in her head
creeping ripping and shredding
like a recording needle

now there's a river
wound up in the Victrola
all dog-eared

with anticipation

Chapin Wilson

When you go outside
for the first time
timidity turns quickly reckless
like sobriety and virginity
and the last thing
you could possibly imagine
is choosing to put on a funeral
dark suit. Unless of course
you were a mod at heart
like the boys in Dr. Feelgood!

David Wilson

BOB DYLAN HAS DIED

Bob Dylan has got me thinking about death again.
Every morning when I check the news I think:
this could be the day. Bob isn't going to live forever.
I imagine the coverage, the tweets,
the outpouring of adoration from those who,
for the last twenty years, have been saying
he can't sing. He's lost a step. Maybe he wasn't
all that special after all.

It's a way of thinking about my own death, isn't it?
I've been doing this more and more lately
particularly since that night last year when I ate
edibles and lay in bed thinking about how
death isn't an abstraction, it's a reality, and that when it comes
it will be like turning off a light and leaving a room in total
darkness.
That is to say it will make everything I've ever loved
or worried about not just pointless, really. Meaningless?
Negated?
It's not quite that either.
It's that it will end.

Of course, Bob's already sussed all of this out:
he not busy being born is busy dying, and all of that. Or:
Death is Not the End, if you're looking for some comfort.
I think of this whenever the shadow creeps across my mind,
and I push it back, or at least I try to. This latest effort is
different, though.
Maybe it's just that it's a new year. There are new possibilities,
sure,

but I've been through enough new years to know that nothing
really changes except that we grow older. If you've got a mind
for science, you know that the world is moving towards high entropy,
the only thing we can rely on is more disorder. This is the 1st or 2nd law
of thermodynamics, I don't recall which. I could google it
and find out, but I've promised myself that I'd do this less this year.
And if I did google it, maybe I'd see the news: Bob Dylan has died.
If not today, then someday, and probably soon.
And then I'd spend the day watching video of Bob
like I've put his life on fast forward. Here he is, baby-faced
but with a mercurial look in his eye, playing his 1930s
Gibson Nick Lucas Special like the reincarnation
of some poet from the Romantic Period.
Here he is in 1974, the year I was born, singing
Knocking on Heaven's Door with The Band in Toronto
after an 8 year hiatus from touring.
Here, at the end of the 20th century,
only months after nearly dying
from pericarditis, singing
Trying to Get to Heaven like some
biblical prophet
in exile.

David Wilson

CIVIL WAR PHOTO

President Lincoln standing stiffly
at Antietam, October, 1862,
flanked by two men
who look off in different directions
though both have their right hands
beneath their coats, over their hearts.
There is a tent behind them;
a rope tied to a tent-post,
extends over Lincoln's head
and is secured by a spike
in the bottom left of the frame.
It is the rope that catches the camera's focus
not Lincoln's face, which is blurry,
wraithlike, though at the moment of this photo
his own death is still three years away.
Still, there is something about Lincoln
that suggests death.
A month earlier, just days before
issuing the Emancipation Proclamation,
nearly 24,000 men died within miles
of where he stands. Lincoln and his wife
had already buried two of their own sons.
The oldest was 11.
A man so surrounded by death
is a man consumed with death.
At Antietam Lincoln had seen trench graves,
had seen the stacked bodies of the Confederate dead,
had seen fathers who had come
to collect their son's bodies.
Looking into the faces of the dead
was like looking at his own boys.
How could he view this and not see death

as anything but the end?
He was not a religious man,
so there was no comfort to be found there.
At the moment of the photograph
he is not looking away
from death, like the man on his left,
or, like the man on his right, slouching
embarrassed in the face of it.
No, he stands pencil-straight,
square-shouldered,
looking at it directly.
All of this captured in the blurred face
of Lincoln at Antietam.

David Wilson

SOMETHING RICH AND STRANGE

I dreamt that you came to me
at night. We were in the field
behind your mother's house.
You were holding a basket
filled with turnips, ginger,
shallots. You were silhouetted
by moonlight so that strands
of your hair fanned out
from your head
like wild flames.

When I awoke in our bed
it was as if I had risen
from the grave; that is to say
as if I had emerged from the ground,
risen into consciousness.

All day I carried with me
the image of you in the field,
the strange sensation
that I had sunken into
something rich and strange
and returned with a prize
I could carry with me,
like an oyster hiding
an illuminated pearl.
I didn't mention it to you.
I kept it to myself.

That evening, in the kitchen,
you stood at the sink

I could see the moon
above your shoulder, outside
the window. I'm so tired,
you said. You turned
towards me. You were holding
a freshly washed turnip.